Descendants of Mathias Ardis

Generation 1

1. **MATHIAS[1] ARDIS** was born in Oct 1724 in Germany. He died on 09 Sep 1781 in Savannah, Georgia. He married Christina Zinn, daughter of Gerhardt Zinn and Margaretha Guth about 1755 in Flat Creek, South Carolina. She was born in 1725 in Neustadt, Germany. She died on 06 May 1785 in Beech Island, South Carolina.

Mathias Ardis and Christina Zinn had the following children:

2.   i.   ISAAC[2] ARDIS was born in 1761 in Flat Creek, South Carolina. He died in 1795 in Beech Island, South Carolina. He married Mary Howell, daughter of Nathaniel Howell and Ann Nail about 1793 in Edgefield County, South Carolina. She was born in 1762. She died on 20 Nov 1795 in Beech Island, South Carolina.

3.   ii. MARY ARDIS was born in 1756 in Flat Creek, South Carolina. She died in 1804. She married (1) JOHN BRADLEY about 1771 in Beech Island, South Carolina. He was born on 19 Jan 1755. He died in 1782 in Savannah, Georgia. She married JOHN DEYAMPERT. He was born in 1755.

         iii. MATTHIAS ARDIS was born about 1757 in Flat Creek, South Carolina.

         iv. ELIZABETH ARDIS was born about 1758 in Flat Creek, South Carolina. She died before Oct 1783. She married FRANCIS CARLISLE.

         v. JOHN ARDIS was born about 1759 in Flat Creek, South Carolina. He died before Oct 1783 in South Carolina.

         vi. JACOB ARDIS was born in 1763 in Flat Creek, South Carolina. He died in 1784 in South Carolina.

4.   vii. SARAH ARDIS was born in 1765 in Flat Creek, South Carolina. She died after 1827. She married BENJAMIN BOWERS. She married PARTAIN PURDUE.

5.   viii. ABRAHAM ARDIS was born in 1767 in New Windsor, South Carolina. He died on 30 May 1817 in Beech Island, , South Carolina. He married (1) SUSANNAH SHINHOLSER, daughter of John Shinholser and Susannah Hiles about 1790 in Beach Island, South Carolina. She was born in 1774. She died on 15 Mar 1807 in Beech Island, , South Carolina. He married (2) SARAH ROSE MARY ZUBLEY on 27 Apr 1809. She was born in 1773. She died on 03 Apr 1836 in Beech Island, , South Carolina.

         ix. DANIEL ARDIS was born about 1768 in New Windsor, South Carolina.

         x. DAVID ARDIS was born in 1773 in New Windsor, South Carolina. He died on 17 Oct 1800 in Beech Island, , South Carolina. He married ELEANOR (UNKNOWN).

Generation 2

2. **ISAAC[2] ARDIS** (Mathias[1]) was born in 1761 in Flat Creek, South Carolina. He died in 1795 in Beech Island, South Carolina. He married Mary Howell, daughter of Nathaniel Howell and Ann Nail about 1793 in Edgefield County, South Carolina. She was born in 1762. She died on 20 Nov 1795 in Beech Island, South Carolina.

More About Isaac Ardis:
Burial: Beech Island, South Carolina
Military Service: Revolutionary War, South Carolina Militia

More About Mary Howell:
Burial: Beech Island, South Carolina

Isaac Ardis and Mary Howell had the following child:

6. i. JOHN[3] ARDIS was born on 01 Dec 1793 in Beech Island, South Carolina. He died on 04 Aug 1878 in Greenville, Alabama. He married (1) MARTHA STALLINGS, daughter of Malachi Stallings and Martha Moseley on 11 Aug 1811 in Greene County, Georgia. She was born on 08 Feb 1787 in York County, South Carolina. She died on 18 Nov 1855 in Salem, Alabama. He married (2) MARY JANE TRAMMEL on 16 Dec 1856 in Butler County, Alabama. She was born on 06 Jan 1829 in Georgia. She died in Feb 1901 in Van Buren County, Arkansas.

3. MARY[2] ARDIS (Mathias[1]) was born in 1756 in Flat Creek, South Carolina. She died in 1804. She married (1) JOHN BRADLEY about 1771 in Beech Island, South Carolina. He was born on 19 Jan 1755. He died in 1782 in Savannah, Georgia. She married JOHN DEYAMPERT. He was born in 1755.

John Bradley and Mary Ardis had the following children:

 i. JAMES[3] BRADLEY was born about 1772 in Beech Island, , South Carolina.

 ii. JOHN ARDIS BRADLEY was born on 04 Sep 1773. He died on 02 Aug 1828 in Georgia. He married Margaret Jameson Meriwether on 24 Jun 1798 in Georgia.

 iii. ISAAC BRADLEY was born about 1775 in Beech Island, , South Carolina.

4. SARAH[2] ARDIS (Mathias[1]) was born in 1765 in Flat Creek, South Carolina. She died after 1827. She married BENJAMIN BOWERS. She married PARTAIN PURDUE.

Benjamin Bowers and Sarah Ardis had the following children:

7. i. HARRIETT[3] BOWERS. She married William P. Fernander on 14 Aug 1813 in Richmond County, Georgia. He was born about 1789. He died in Jun 1849 in Coweta County, Georgia.

 ii. MARY BOWERS. She married JACOB ZINN.

5. ABRAHAM[2] ARDIS (Mathias[1]) was born in 1767 in New Windsor, South Carolina. He died on 30 May 1817 in Beech Island, , South Carolina. He married (1) SUSANNAH SHINHOLSER, daughter of John Shinholser and Susannah Hiles about 1790 in Beach Island, South Carolina. She was born in 1774. She died on 15 Mar 1807 in Beech Island, , South Carolina. He married (2) SARAH ROSE MARY ZUBLEY on 27 Apr 1809. She was born in 1773. She died on 03 Apr 1836 in Beech Island, , South Carolina.

More About Abraham Ardis:
Burial: Beech Island, South Carolina

More About Susannah Shinholser:
Burial: Beech Island, ,South Carolina

Abraham Ardis and Susannah Shinholser had the following children:

8. i. MATTHIAS[3] ARDIS was born in 1791 in Beech Island, , South Carolina. He died in Mt. Lebanon, Louisiana. He married Louisa Nail, daughter of Casper Nail about 1822 in Beach Island, South Carolina. She was born about 1801 in Edgefield County, South Carolina. She died in Mt. Lebanon, Louisiana.

 ii. MARY ARDIS was born about 1793 in Beech Island, , South Carolina. She married

Arthur Simpkins on 11 Dec 1813 in Beach Island, South Carolina.

    iii.   JOHN ARDIS was born about 1795 in Beech Island, , South Carolina. He died in 1825 in Beech Island, , South Carolina.

    iv.   ELIZA ARDIS was born on 08 Aug 1800 in Beech Island, , South Carolina. She died on 30 Jun 1837 in Beech Island, , South Carolina. She married John Milledge Galphin on 09 Dec 1819 in Beach Island, South Carolina.

    v.   ABRAHAM ARDIS was born in Aug 1802 in Beech Island, , South Carolina. He died in Feb 1837 in Beech Island, , South Carolina. He married SARAH NAIL.

    vi.   ROSE HANNAH SOPHIA ARDIS was born in 1804 in Beech Island, , South Carolina. She married CASPER NAIL.

    vii.   DAVID ARDIS was born in 1806 in Beech Island, , South Carolina.

More About Sarah Rose Mary Zubley:
Burial: Beech Island, South Carolina

Abraham Ardis and Sarah Rose Mary Zubley had the following child:

    viii.   HENRY ZUBLEY ARDIS was born on 08 Aug 1811 in Beech Island, , South Carolina. He died on 18 Aug 1881 in Edgefield County, South Carolina. He married ANNA W. BIGGS. He married ELIZABETH COOKSEY.

Generation 3

6.   JOHN[3] ARDIS (Isaac[2], Mathias[1]) was born on 01 Dec 1793 in Beech Island, South Carolina. He died on 04 Aug 1878 in Greenville, Alabama. He married (1) MARTHA STALLINGS, daughter of Malachi Stallings and Martha Moseley on 11 Aug 1811 in Greene County, Georgia. She was born on 08 Feb 1787 in York County, South Carolina. She died on 18 Nov 1855 in Salem, Alabama. He married (2) MARY JANE TRAMMEL on 16 Dec 1856 in Butler County, Alabama. She was born on 06 Jan 1829 in Georgia. She died in Feb 1901 in Van Buren County, Arkansas.

More About John
Ardis:
b: 01 Dec 1793
Burial: Pioneer Cemetery, Greenville, Alabama
Living In: 1820 Putnam County, Georgia
Living In: 1840 Russell County, Alabama
Living In: 1850 Russell County, Alabama
Living In: 1866 in Butler County, Alabama
Living In: 1870 Greenville, Butler County, Alabama
Occupation: 1850 in Russell County, Alabama; Farmer
Property: 1850 in Russell County, Alabama; 220 Acres Improved and 140 Acres Unimproved

More About Martha Stallings:
b: 08 Feb 1787
Burial: Salem, Alabama

John Ardis and Martha Stallings had the following children:

9.   i.   MARY ANN MCCOY[4] ARDIS was born on 30 Mar 1812 in Greene County, Georgia. She died on 16 Jan 1850 in Harris County, Georgia. She married Stephen C. Pace, son of William Pace and Mary May on 10 Jul 1827 in Putnam County, Georgia. He was born on 11 Jul 1802 in South Carolina. He died on 14 Apr 1872 in Creek Stand, Macon County, Alabama.

10.   ii. ISAAC ARDIS was born in 1816 in Greene County, Georgia. He died in 1870 in Sulphur Springs, Texas. He married Jane Elizabeth White, daughter of Johnathan White and Elizabeth (unknown) on 19 Oct 1842 in Russell County, Alabama. She was born on 27 Aug 1825 in Meriwether County, Georgia. She died on 21 Sep 1905 in Strawn, Texas.

11.   iii. ARCHIBALD MCCOY ARDIS was born on 28 Aug 1818 in Putnam County, Georgia. He died on 02 May 1859 in Greenville, Alabama. He married Joanna Leticia White, daughter of Johnathan White and Elizabeth (unknown) on 28 Feb 1842 in Russell County, Alabama. She was born in 1826 in Oglethorpe, Georgia.

12.   iv. CAROLINE COLUMBIA SARAH ANN COLLINGSWORTH ARDIS was born on 18 Nov 1821 in Putnam County, Georgia. She died on 21 Feb 1910 in Corsicana, Navarro County, Texas. She married John Pace, son of William Pace and Mary May on 02 Feb 1835 in Harris County, Georgia. He was born on 09 Dec 1809 in Putnam County, Georgia. He died on 17 Nov 1879 in Corsicana, Navarro County, Texas.

    v.   JULIUS ARDIS was born about 1820 in Putnam County, Georgia.

13.   vi. JOHN COLUMBUS ARDIS was born on 31 Aug 1823 in Putnam County, Georgia. He died on 24 Dec 1877 in Downey, California. He married Frances Amanda Harris, daughter of Britain D. Harris and Sarah A. Walton on 17 Apr 1848 in Russell County, Alabama. She was born on 23 Nov 1831 in Alabama. She died on 01 Dec 1902 in Downey, California.

14.   vii. MARTHA ALY D. ARDIS was born on 25 Apr 1825 in Putnam County, Georgia. She died on 07 Aug 1906 in Vernon Parish, Louisiana. She married (1) ANDERSON V. ALLEN about 1844 in Russell County, Alabama. He was born about 1821 in Russell County, Alabama. He died on 20 Nov 1846. She married (2) CHARNER T. SCAIFE on 01 Mar 1848 in Russell County, Alabama. He was born about 1823 in South Carolina. He died on 09 Jun 1858 in Atlanta, Georgia.

15.   viii. ELIZABETH ARDIS was born in 1828 in Columbus, Georgia. She died before 10 Jul 1860. She married George W. Adair, son of John D. Adair and Mary P. (unknown) on 20 Jul 1847 in Russell County, Alabama. He was born in 1829 in Gwinnett County, Georgia.

    ix.   WILEY HAMIL ARDIS was born on 08 May 1830 in Columbus, Georgia. He died on 22 Jan 1892 in Carthage, Panola County, Texas. He married (1) FRANCES L. MILLER, daughter of John Miller on 09 Nov 1848 in Chambers County, Alabama. She was born in 1829 in Georgia. She died on 30 Mar 1885 in Texas. He married (2) DEMETSIA J. HIGGINS on 12 Jul 1887 in Panola County, Texas.

More About Wiley Hamil Ardis:
Burial: Athens Cemetery, Athens, Henderson County, Texas
Occupation: 1850 in Russell County, Alabama; Farmer
Occupation: 1860 in Butler County, Alabama; Preacher
Occupation:1870 in Fincastle, Henderson County, Texas; Minister of the Gospel
Occupation: 1880 in Fincastle, Henderson County, Texas; Minister
Military Service: Bet. 05 Apr-12 Aug 1862 ; Company E, 2nd Alabama Cavalry, C.S.A.

Notes for Wiley Hamil Ardis:
Enlisted in Company E, 2nd Alabama Cavalry at Bethel Church in Butler County,
Alabama on April 5, 1862 as a private. Mustered in at Camp Stone on May 6,
1862. Horse valued at $300 by enlistment Officer at time of enlistment.
Became Chaplain of 2nd Alabama Cavalry on May 2, 1862.
Resigned his commision as Chaplain due to health on August 12, 1862.

1880 U.S. census shows Florence Early as an adopted daughter of Wiley and
Frances Ardis and gives her name as Florence H. Ardis. Death certificate for
Florence gives her name as Florence Early Grimes (wife of Edwin W. Grimes)
and gives her parents names as Walter C. Early and Virginia F. Wilkinson.

More About Mary Jane Trammel:
Living In: 1880 Starlington, Butler County, Alabama
Living In: 1900 Living with her son, William Ardis, and his family in Davis, Van Buren County,
Arkansas.

More About John Ardis and Mary Jane Trammel:
Marriage Fact: Married by Judge of Probate S.J. Holling

John Ardis and Mary Jane Trammel had the following children:

16.   x. NEBRASKA KANSAS ARDIS was born on 22 Oct 1857 in Greeneville, Alabama. He died on
18 Feb 1933 in Perdido, Alabama. He married (1) MARY JANE ODOM, daughter of
Jethro J. Odom and Martha Ellis on 19 Apr 1878 in Greeneville, Butler County,
Alabama. She was born on 02 Oct 1860 in Greeneville, Alabama. She died on 28 Feb
1917 in Perdido, Alabama. He married (2) LILLIE CHAMBLESS, daughter of David
Chambless and Frances M. Avery on 16 Jun 1917 in Perdido, Baldwin County,
Alabama. She was born on 31 Dec 1895 in Perdido, Alabama. She died on 22 Apr
1986 in Spanish Fort, Alabama.

       xi. BASCOMBE K. ARDIS was born in Oct 1859 in Greeneville, Alabama.

More About Bascombe K. Ardis:
Living In: 1880 Living with his mother in Starlington, Butler County, Alabama
Occupation: 1900 in Center Post, Cleburne County, Arkansas; Farmer

       xii. HENRY T. ARDIS was born in 1863 in Greenville, Alabama. He died about 1882
in Greenville, Alabama.

       xiii. ARIZONA ARDIS was born in 1865 in Greenville, Alabama. She died about 1876
in Greeneville, Alabama.

17.   xiv. WILLIAM TRAMMELL ARDIS was born in Feb 1867 in Greenville, Alabama. He died in
1944 in Escambia County, Florida. He married (1) SARDELIA WHITTLE on 24 Apr 1886
in Monroe County, Alabama. She was born in Jul 1864 in Mobile, Alabama. She died
in 1926. He married (2) ELLEN PATE on 05 Mar 1926 in Brewton County, Alabama.
She was born on 01 Jun 1876 in Florida. She died on 15 Dec 1932 in Century,
Escambia County, Florida. He married (3) FLORENCE PEST on 16 Apr 1933. He
married (4) VERA ARGO on 01 Apr 1939. She was born about 1903 in

Tennessee.

7. **HARRIETT**[3] **BOWERS** (Sarah[2] Ardis, Mathias[1] Ardis, Benjamin). She married William P. Fernander on 14 Aug 1813 in Richmond County, Georgia. He was born about 1789. He died in Jun 1849 in Coweta County, Georgia.

    William P. Fernander and Harriett Bowers had the following children:

    i.   EVALINE E.[4] FERNANDER was born about 1820. She died before 1870 in Lafayette County, Mississippi. She married Hezekiah D. McInosh on 24 Oct 1838 in Fayette County, Georgia.

    ii. ELIZABETH A. FERNANDER was born in Jul 1821. She died on 27 Feb 1822 in Richmond County, Georgia.

    iii. MATTHIAS FERNANDER was born about 1822.

    iv. AMANDA A. FERNANDER was born about 1825. She married Marshall Morton on 23 Nov 1847 in Coweta County, Georgia.

    v.   WILLIAM SAMUEL FERNANDER was born about 1832.

8. **MATTHIAS**[3] **ARDIS** (Abraham[2], Mathias[1]) was born in 1791 in Beech Island, , South Carolina. He died in Mt. Lebanon, Louisiana. He married Louisa Nail, daughter of Casper Nail about 1822 in Beach Island, South Carolina. She was born about 1801 in Edgefield County, South Carolina. She died in Mt. Lebanon, Louisiana.

    More About Matthias Ardis:
    Burial: Mt. Lebanon, Louisiana

    More About Louisa Nail: Burial:
    Mt. Lebanon, Louisiana

    Matthias Ardis and Louisa Nail had the following children:

    i.   SUSAN REBECCA[4] ARDIS was born on 03 Jul 1823 in Beech Island, , South Carolina. She died on 21 Mar 1908 in Mt. Lebanon, Louisiana. She married J.C. Egan on 07 Sep 1852 in Mt. Lebanon, Louisiana.

    ii.   LUCIOUS ARDIS was born in 1825 in Beech Island, , South Carolina.

    iii. CLINTON H. ARDIS was born in 1827 in Beech Island, , South Carolina. He married Harriet L. Hamilton on 18 Dec 1850 in Madison County, Mississippi.

    iv.   SARAH LOUISA ARDIS was born in 1830 in Beech Island, , South Carolina. She died on 19 Aug 1857 in Mt. Lebanon, Louisiana.

    v.   CASPER ARDIS was born in 1833 in Beech Island, , South Carolina.

    vi.   HARRIET H. ARDIS was born in 1835 in Beech Island, , South Carolina.

    vii. JOHN B. ARDIS was born in 1840 in Beech Island, , South Carolina. He married Mary M. Petty on 06 Feb 1873 in Hopkins County, Texas.

9. **MARY ANN MCCOY**[4] **ARDIS** (John[3], Isaac[2], Mathias[1]) was born on 30 Mar 1812 in Greene County, Georgia. She died on 16 Jan 1850 in Harris County, Georgia. She married Stephen C. Pace, son of William Pace and Mary May on 10 Jul 1827 in Putnam County, Georgia. He was born on 11 Jul 1802 in South Carolina. He died on 14 Apr 1872 in Creek Stand, Macon County, Alabama.

More About Mary Ann McCoy Ardis:
Burial: Pace Cemetery, Columbus, Muscogee County, Georgia

More About Stephen C.
Pace: b: 11 Jul 1802
Burial: Creek Stand Cemetery, Creek Stand, Macon County,
Alabama
Occupation: 1850 in Harris County, Georgia; Farmer
Occupation: 1860 in Macon County, Alabama; Farmer
Occupation: 1870 in Warrior Stand, Macon County, Alabama; Farmer

Notes for Stephen C. Pace:
DEATH AND OBITUARY NOTICES FROM THE SOUTHERN CHRISTIAN ADVOCATE Issue of May 8, 1872 -- Stephen Pace died at his residence at Creek Stand, Macon county, Ala., April 14th 1872. Brother Pace was born in Edgefield District, South Carolina, July 11th 1802. his father removed to Putnam county, Ga., when he was a child. In 1828, brother Pace moved to Harris county, Ga., where he remained until 1854, when he removed to the place where he died.

Stephen C. Pace and Mary Ann McCoy Ardis had the following children:

i.   THOMAS M.[5] PACE was born in Jun 1828 in Georgia. He died in 1910 in Polk County, Georgia. He married (1) MARY K. BURT on 29 Jan 1850 in Harris County, Georgia. She was born in 1832. She died in 1874 in Georgia. He married (2) MARY FLETCHER PITTS on 17 Dec 1874 in Harris County, Georgia. She was born in Jul 1840 in Georgia.

More About Thomas M. Pace:
Occupation: 1850 in Harris County, Georgia; Farmer
Occupation: 1860 in Macon County, Alabama; Farmer
Occupation: 1870 in Cedartown, Polk County, Georgia; Farmer
Occupation:1880 in Cedartown, Polk County, Georgia; Dry Goods Merchant
Occupation: 1900 in Cedartown, Polk County, Georgia; Farmer
Occupation:1910 in Cedartown, Polk County, Georgia; Retired

ii. MARY MCCOY PACE was born on 10 Feb 1831 in Georgia. She died on 28 Jun 1857 in Georgia. She married (1) A. O. SCAEF on 02 Oct 1849 in Harris County, Georgia. She married WILLIAM A. CHAMBLISS.

iii. MARTHA ARDIS PACE was born about 1832 in Georgia.

iv. SARAH ELIZABETH PACE was born on 21 Oct 1834 in Georgia.

v.   JOHN WILLIAM PACE was born in Jul 1836 in Georgia. He died on 17 Aug 1911 in Hurtsboro, Russell County, Alabama. He married (1) SARAH A. V. DAWKINS, daughter of Reuben Dawkins and Elizabeth (unknown) on 10 Jun 1858 in Russell County, Alabama. She was born on 08 Oct 1839 in Alabama. She died on 02 Feb

1885. He married (2) ANNA ELIZABETH DANIEL, daughter of Andrew J. Daniel on 26 Jun 1885 in Carroll County, Georgia. She was born in Apr 1865 in Georgia. She died on 01 Aug 1938 in Hurtboro, Russell County, Alabama.

More About John William Pace:
Living In: 1908 Russell County, Alabama
Occupation: 1860 in Macon County, Alabama; Farmer
Occupation: 1870 in Warrior Stand, Macon County, Alabama; Farmer
Occupation: 1880 in Auburn, Lee County, Alabama; Farmer
Occupation: 1880 in Auburn, Lee County, Alabama; Farmer
Occupation: 1900 in Warrior Stand, Macon County, Alabama; Farmer
Occupation: 1910 in Hurtsboro, Russell County, Alabama; Retired
Military Service: Company C, 3rd Alabama Infantry, C.S.A.

   vi.   LUCY AMELIA PACE was born about 1838 in Georgia.

   vii.   ISAAC STEPHEN PACE was born about 1839 in Georgia.

   viii.   GEORGIA ANN PACE was born about 1846 in Georgia.

   ix.   ANNA PACE was born on 20 Aug 1849 in Harris County, Georgia. She died on 25 Oct 1929 in Tuskegee, Macon County, Alabama. She married JOSEPH J. FORT.

      More About Anna Pace:
      Burial: 26 Oct 1929 in Tuskegee City Cemetery, Tuskegee, Macon County, Alabama

10.   **ISAAC⁴ ARDIS** (John³, Isaac², Mathias¹) was born in 1816 in Greene County, Georgia. He died in 1870 in Sulphur Springs, Texas. He married Jane Elizabeth White, daughter of Johnathan White and Elizabeth (unknown) on 19 Oct 1842 in Russell County, Alabama. She was born on 27 Aug 1825 in Meriwether County, Georgia. She died on 21 Sep 1905 in Strawn, Texas.

More About Isaac Ardis:
Living In: 1840 Russell County, Alabama
Occupation: 1850 in Russell County, Alabama; Farmer
Occupation: 1860 in Pike County, Alabama; Farmer
Property: 1850 in Russell County, Alabama; 200 Acres Improved and 120 Acres Unimproved

Notes for Isaac Ardis:
Became a Mason at Brightstar Lodge number 221 in Sulphur Springs, Texas on December 3, 1868. Obituary for his wife states that Isaac died in 1870, indicating that it was probably early 1870. Isaac is not with his wife and children on the 1870 U.S. census for Hopkins County, Texas dated August 17, 1870.

Isaac Ardis died in 1870 before August 17, 1870 when the 1870 U.S. census for Precinct 1, Hopkins County, Texas was enumerated.

More About Jane Elizabeth White:
Burial: Mount Marion Cemetery, Strawn, Texas
Living In: 1870 Hopkins County, Texas on the farm of Thomas Beard
Living In: 1900 Young County, Texas with her son Julius C. Ardis and family.

Occupation: 1880 in Hopkins County, Texas; Farmer

Notes for Jane Elizabeth White:

   Strawn, Tex., Sept. 21 - Mrs. E.J. Ardis died at the residence of A.N. Edwards this morning at 8 o'clock. Deceased was 80 years old and had lived in Texas many years. She leaves eight children, Dr. I. Ardis of Greenville, three sons at Eliasville, two sons at Sulphur Springs, Mrs. T. Marshall of Indian Territory, and Mrs. A.N. Edwards of this place." 23 Sep 1905, The Dallas Morning News, page 7.

More About Isaac Ardis and Jane Elizabeth White:
Marriage License: 19 Oct 1842 in Russell County, Alabama
Marriage Fact: 28 Feb 1842; Marriage Bond signed
Marriage Fact: Married by John W. Tally, M.G.

Isaac Ardis and Jane Elizabeth White had the following children:

 i. JOHN C. [5] ARDIS was born on 11 Mar 1843 in Salem, Alabama. He died on 06 Sep 1858 in Pike County, Alabama.

 ii. JULIUS CAESAR ARDIS was born in 1845 in Salem, Alabama. He died in 1863 in Iuka, Tishomingo County, Mississippi.

 More About Julius Caesar Ardis:
 Military Service: Bet. 10 Jan-17 Nov 1863 ; Company E, 53rd Alabama Mounted Infantry, C.S.A.

18. iii. JOANNA COLUMBIA ARDIS was born on 04 Feb 1847 in Salem, Alabama. She died on 8 Aug 1922 in Greenville, Texas. She married Ambrose Newton Edwards, son of Ambrose Edwards and Emeline James Gaulding on 05 Dec 1865 in Dale County, Alabama. He was born on 21 Oct 1840 in Russell County, Alabama. He died on 20 Jul 1933 in Strawn, Texas.

19. iv. JOHNATHAN WHITE ARDIS was born in Apr 1850 in Salem, Alabama. He died on 11 May 1917 in San Antonio, Bexar County, Texas. He married Rosa Lee Brinker on 21 Nov 1875 in Sulphur Springs, Texas. She was born in Apr 1853 in Shelby County, Alabama. She died on 27 Jun 1919 in Sulphur Springs, Hopkins County, Texas.

20. v. ISAAC ARDIS was born on 16 Dec 1851 in Salem, Alabama. He died on 13 Apr 1913 in Greenville, Texas. He married Martha J. Taylor, daughter of Alexander Taylor and Margaret Davis on 05 Dec 1875 in Hunt County, Texas. She was born on 18 Oct 1843 in Marshall County, Tennessee. She died on 07 Feb 1923 in Greenville, Texas.

21. vi. ROBERT HENRY ARDIS was born on 21 Jan 1854 in Salem, Alabama. He died on 17 Dec 1932 in Eliasville, Texas. He married Amanda A. Wells, daughter of William Wells and (unknown) Carver on 27 Dec 1877 in Sulphur Springs, Texas. She was born on 11 Mar 1859 in Sulphur Springs, Texas. She died on 26 Oct 1926 in Eliasville, Texas.

22. vii. WILLIAM HOWARD ARDIS was born on 23 Apr 1856 in Pike County, Alabama. He died on 18 Sep 1924 in Eliasville, Texas. He married Edna Earl Collins, daughter of

Henry Clay Collins and Mary Ann Darwin in 1885 in Greenville, Hopkins County, Texas. She was born on 07 Apr 1868 in Tennessee. She died on 09 Jan 1907 in Eliasville, Texas.

   viii. JOHN C. ARDIS was born on 11 Dec 1858 in Pike County, Alabama. He died on 09 Oct 1860 in Pike County, Alabama.

23.   ix. JAMES E. ARDIS was born on 09 Jul 1861 in Westville, Alabama. He died on 24 Sep 1934 in Sulphur Springs, Texas. He married Clistia Ellen Chapin, daughter of Paul Stilman Chapin and Matilda (unknown) on 22 Aug 1883 in Sulphur Springs, Texas. She was born on 22 Aug 1866 in Sulphur Springs, Texas. She died on 24 Mar 1934 in Sulphur Springs, Texas.

24.   x. JULIUS CAESAR ARDIS was born on 02 Feb 1864 in Westville, Alabama. He died on 14 Jul 1937 in Breckenridge, Stephans County, Texas. He married Cora Densmore, daughter of Samuel M. Densmore and Margaret C. (unknown) on 18 Nov 1895 in Eliasville, Texas. She was born on 20 Jan 1870 in Greene County, Tennessee. She died on 17 Nov 1910 in Eliasville, Texas.

25.   xi. MARTHA INEZ ARDIS was born on 09 Aug 1866 in Greenville, Alabama. She died on 23 Jun 1911 in Lamar County, Texas. She married Thomas H. Marshall, son of John L.Marshall and Susan A. (unknown) on 05 Dec 1883 in Lamar County, Texas. He was born in Aug 1863 in Arkansas.

11. **ARCHIBALD MCCOY**[4] **ARDIS** (John[3], Isaac[2], Mathias[1]) was born on 28 Aug 1818 in Putnam County, Georgia. He died on 02 May 1859 in Greenville, Alabama. He married Joanna Leticia White, daughter of Johnathan White and Elizabeth (unknown) on 28 Feb 1842 in Russell County, Alabama. She was born in 1826 in Oglethorpe, Georgia.

More About Archibald McCoy
Ardis: Burial: Greenville, Alabama
Occupation: 1850 in Russell County, Alabama; Farmer
Property: 1850 in Russell County, Alabama; 100 Acres Improved and 80 Acres Unimproved

Notes for Archibald McCoy Ardis:
Living in Russell County, Alabama in

1850.

More About Joanna Leticia White:

Living In: 1860 Living in Pike County, Alabama next door to her brother in law, Isaac Ardis.
Living In: 1870 Joanna and her children (John, Isaac and Henry) are living with her son in law, Young Mansfield Edwards, in Hopkins County, Texas

Archibald McCoy Ardis and Joanna Leticia White had the following children:

   i. MARTHA E .[5] ARDIS was born on 25 Feb 1843 in Russell County, Alabama. She died on 27 Jan 1903 in Brazoria County, Texas. She married (1) YOUNG MANSFIELD EDWARDS, son of Ambrose Edwards and Emeline James Gaulding on 05 Dec 1865 in Dale County, Alabama. He was born in May 1843 in Russell County, Alabama. He died on 22 Feb 1923 in Sulphur Springs, Hopkins County, Texas. She married (2) WILLIAM B. MOORE on 18 Oct 1860 in Pike County, Alabama. He was born about 1837. He died on 24 May 1862 in Lynchburg, Virginia.

    More About Martha E. Ardis:

Burial: City Cemetery, Sulphur Springs, Texas, 1C, Lot 39

Notes for Martha E. Ardis:
Filed a claim with the Confederate War Department on November 17, 1863 for the loss of her husband, William B. Moore.

----

26.   ii. THOMAS ARCHIBALD ARDIS was born on 03 May 1845 in Salem, Alabama. He died on 18 Feb 1889 in Harrison County, Texas. He married Sarah J. Long, daughter of James D Long and Blanch Ann (unknown) on 08 Nov 1866 in Dale County, Alabama. She was born on 28 May 1846 in Muscogee County, Georgia. She died on 04 Jul 1925 in Ore City, Upshur County, Texas.

27.   iii. JOHN BLOOMER ARDIS was born on 23 Dec 1847 in Salem, Alabama. He died on 28 Feb 1900 in Hopkins County, Texas. He married Mary Elizabeth Elliott, daughter of John P. Elliott and Jane Ann Lewis on 24 Dec 1876 in Sulphur Springs, Texas. She was born on 19 Dec 1859 in Hopkins County, Texas. She died on 06 Jun 1899 in Hopkins County, Texas.

28.   iv. ISAAC HAMIL ARDIS was born in Jul 1852 in Salem, Alabama. He died on 14 Feb 1919 in Sulphur Springs, Texas. He married Martha Dennis McCorkle, daughter of Logan Henderson McCorkle and Isabella Zardanik Harper Brown on 24 Dec 1876 in Sulphur Springs, Texas. She was born on 17 Nov 1860 in Hopkins County, Texas. She died on 14 Oct 1934 in Sulphur Springs, Hopkins County, Texas.

29.   v. HENRY LOVE ARDIS was born on 12 Sep 1857 in Pike County, Alabama. He died on 6 Jan 1927 in Sulphur Springs, Texas. He married Martha Pate, daughter of John W. Pate and Sarah A. Wester on 02 Dec 1880 in Sulphur Springs, Texas. She was born on 20 Sep 1863 in Hopkins County, Texas. She died on 27 Jan 1952 in Sulphur Springs, Texas.

12.   CAROLINE COLUMBIA SARAH ANN COLLINGSWORTH[4] ARDIS (John[3], Isaac[2], Mathias[1]) was born on 18 Nov 1821 in Putnam County, Georgia. She died on 21 Feb 1910 in Corsicana, Navarro County, Texas. She married John Pace, son of William Pace and Mary May on 02 Feb 1835 in Harris County, Georgia. He was born on 09 Dec 1809 in Putnam County, Georgia. He died on 17 Nov 1879 in Corsicana, Navarro County, Texas.

More About Caroline Columbia Sarah Ann Collingsworth Ardis:
Burial: 22 Feb 1910 in Ennis, Ellis County, Texas
Living In: 05 Jun 1880 Caroline and her daughter, Martha, are living with Caroline's son, John Ardis Pace, in Ellis County, Texas
Living In: 09 Jun 1880 Caroline and her daughter, Martha, are living with Caroline's son, Stephen A. Pace, in Corsicana, Texas

More About John Pace:
b: 07 Dec 1809
Burial: Myrtle Cemetery, Ennis, Ellis County, Texas
Cause Of Death: Typhoid Fever
Occupation: 1850 in Muscogee County, Georgia; Farmer
Occupation: 1860 in Russell County, Alabama; Farmer
Occupation: 1870 in Salem, Lee County, Alabama; Farmer

John Pace and Caroline Columbia Sarah Ann Collingsworth Ardis had the following children: 30.

i. JOHN ARDIS[5] PACE was born on 09 Apr 1838 in Harris County, Georgia. He died on

02 Jul 1909 in Ennis, Texas. He married (1) ELIZA FRAZIER on 04 Dec 1860 in Russell County, Alabama. She was born in Alabama. He married (2) LEVINIA R. (UNKNOWN) about 1876. She was born on 12 Dec 1840 in Alabama. She died on 09 Feb 1915 in Ennis, Texas.

      ii.   ELISA PACE was born in 1840 in Harris County, Georgia.

      iii.   WILLIAM A. PACE was born in 1842 in Muscogee County, Alabama.

      iv.   ISAAC E. PACE was born in 1846 in Muscogee County, Alabama.

31.   v. STEPHEN A. PACE was born on 19 Sep 1848 in Columbus, Muscogee County, Georgia. He died on 01 Mar 1921 in Corsicana, Navarro County, Texas. He married Achsah Eugenia Maddux on 05 Dec 1870 in Freestone, Texas. She was born on 26 Aug 1849 in Alabama. She died on 30 Mar 1901 in Corsicana, Navarro County, Texas.

      vi.   MARTHA PACE was born about 1862 in Alabama.

13.   **JOHN COLUMBUS**[4] **ARDIS** (John[3], Isaac[2], Mathias[1]) was born on 31 Aug 1823 in Putnam County, Georgia. He died on 24 Dec 1877 in Downey, California. He married Frances Amanda Harris, daughter of Britain D. Harris and Sarah A. Walton on 17 Apr 1848 in Russell County, Alabama. She was born on 23 Nov 1831 in Alabama. She died on 01 Dec 1902 in Downey, California.

More About John Columbus Ardis:
Burial: Downey District Cemetery, Downey, California
Occupation: 1850 in Russell County, Alabama; Lawyer
Occupation: 1860 in El Dorado, Union County, Arkansas; School Teacher
Occupation: 1870 in Los Nietos, Los Angeles County, California; School Teacher
Occupation: Minister

Notes for John Columbus Ardis:
Graduated from Emory College in Oxford, Georgia in
1846. Licensed to preach by John W. Starr in 1847.
Moved to Union County, Arkansas in 1859.
Ordained a Deacon in the Methodist Episcopal Church, South by Bishop Andrew in 1856. Ordained as elder by Bishop Paine in 1860.
Arrived in Los Angeles County, California in July 1868.

More About Frances Amanda Harris:
Burial: Downey District Cemetery, Downey, California
Living In: 1900 Downey, Los Angeles County, California
Occupation: 1880 in Los Nietos, Los Angeles County, California; Farmer

More About John Columbus Ardis and Frances Amanda
Harris: Marriage Fact: Married by J. Sciafe, M.G.

John Columbus Ardis and Frances Amanda Harris had the following children:

      i.   JOHN DAWSON[5] ARDIS was born on 14 Jan 1849 in Salem, Alabama. He died on 05 Feb 1915 in Pomona, California. He married Ada Virginia Rudd on 02 Nov 1899 in Downey, California. She was born on 25 May 1871 in Harrison County, Iowa. She died on 10 Jul 1964 in Los Angeles County, California.

More About John Dawson Ardis:
Burial: Downey District Cemetery, Downey, California

Notes for John Dawson Ardis:
Headstone gives date of death as 1914 with no day or month.

ii. ISAAC L. ARDIS was born on 30 Apr 1853 in Salem, Alabama. He died on 03 Oct 1903 in Downey, California. He married Josephine Dodson on 05 Jul 1878 in Los Angeles County, California.

More About Isaac L. Ardis:
Burial: Downey District Cemetery, Downey, California
Living In: 1900 Living with his mother in Downey, California.
Occupation: 1900 in Rail Road Engineer; Downey, California

iii. SALLIE A. ARDIS was born on 24 Aug 1858 in Salem, Alabama. She died on 02 Feb 1947. She married A.S. Gray on 16 May 1878 in Downey, California.

iv. LIDA T. ARDIS was born on 27 May 1861 in Eldorado, Arkansas. She died on 27 Mar 1931 in Glendale, California. She married William B. Crawford on 15 Nov 1883 in Los Nietos, California.

More About Lida T. Ardis:
Living In: 1900 Living as a widow with her mother in Downey, California.
Occupation: 1900 in Downey, California; School Teacher

v. JULIUS HARRIS ARDIS was born on 11 May 1863 in Eldorado, Arkansas. He died on 10 Jul 1936 in Downey, California. He married Mamie Haygood on 24 Sep 1889.

Notes for Julius Harris Ardis:
Graduated from Emory College in Oxford, Georgia.

vi. FANNIE ALABAMA ARDIS was born on 27 Oct 1866 in Eldorado, Arkansas. She died on 27 Apr 1894. She married James N. Pemberton on 04 Oct 1888 in Downey, California.

vii. WILLIAM M. ARDIS was born on 23 Oct 1870 in Downey, California. He died on 28 May 1933 in Downey, California. He married SALLY (UNKNOWN).

More About William M. Ardis:
Burial: Downey District Cemetery, Downey, California

viii. JULIA ARDIS was born on 11 Dec 1872 in Downey, California. She died on 28 Jul 1944 in Bellflower, California. She married Joseph M. McCullough on 07 Jun 1894 in Downey, California.

ix. BASCOMB ARDIS was born in 1873 in Downey, California. He died on 05 Jul 1878 in Downey, California.

14. **MARTHA ALY D.**[4] **ARDIS** (John[3], Isaac[2], Mathias[1]) was born on 25 Apr 1825 in Putnam County, Georgia. She died on 07 Aug 1906 in Vernon Parish, Louisiana. She married (1) **ANDERSON V. ALLEN** about 1844 in Russell County, Alabama. He was born about 1821 in Russell County, Alabama. He died on 20 Nov 1846. She married (2) **CHARNER T. SCAIFE** on 01 Mar 1848 in Russell County, Alabama. He was born about 1823 in South Carolina. He died on 09 Jun 1858 in Atlanta, Georgia.

More About Martha Aly D. Ardis:
Burial: Old Leesville Cemetery, Leesville, Vernon Parish, Louisiana
Living In: 1860 Living, with her children, in Salem, Russell County, Alabama.
Living In: 1870 Living, with her children, in Dale County, Alabama
Living In: 1880 Living in Pensacola, Florida in the household of Green Brown, father in law of her son, John Scaife.
Living In: 1900 Living with her son, William Scaife, and his family in Dead Fall, Butler County, Alabama.

Notes for Anderson V. Allen:
Estate probated in Russell County, Alabama. Administrator of his estate was John Ardis.

Anderson V. Allen and Martha Aly D. Ardis had the following child:

    i.   MARTHA[5] ALLEN was born in 1845 in Russell County, Alabama.

More About Charner T. Scaife:
Occupation: 1850 in Russell County, Alabama; Merchant

Charner T. Scaife and Martha Aly D. Ardis had the following children:

    i.   WILEY[5] SCAIFE was born about 1850 in Alabama.

32.   ii. JOHN JESSE SCAIFE was born on 02 May 1852 in Alabama. He died on 20 Apr 1921 in Louisiana. He married ALLIE EALY BROWN. She was born on 10 Oct 1860 in Alabama. She died on 07 Dec 1921 in Louisiana.

    iii.   CHARNER SCAIFE was born about 1855 in Alabama.

    iv.   WILLIAM SCAIFE was born in Feb 1856 in Alabama. He married FRANCES L. (UNKNOWN). She was born in Apr 1870 in Alabama.

    More About William Scaife:
    Occupation: 1900 in Dead Fall, Butler County, Alabama; Farmer

    v.   MARY SCAIFE was born about 1858 in Alabama.

15. **ELIZABETH**[4] **ARDIS** (John[3], Isaac[2], Mathias[1]) was born in 1828 in Columbus, Georgia. She died before 10 Jul 1860. She married George W. Adair, son of John D. Adair and Mary P. (unknown) on 20 Jul 1847 in Russell County, Alabama. He was born in 1829 in Gwinnett County, Georgia.

More About Elizabeth Ardis:
Cause Of Death: ; Consumption (Tuberculosis)

More About George W. Adair:
Occupation: 1850 in Russell County, Alabama; Farmer
Occupation: 1860 in Smackover Township, Ouachita County, Arkansas; Farmer

More About George W. Adair and Elizabeth Ardis:
Marriage Fact: Married by J. Scaife, M.G.

George W. Adair and Elizabeth Ardis had the following children:

 i. AMANDA[5] ADAIR was born in 1848 in Alabama.

   More About Amanda Adair:
   Living In: 10 Jul 1860 Living with her father in Smackover Township, Ouachita County, Arkansas.
   Living In: 06 Sep 1860 Living with her uncle, Isaac Ardis, in Pike County, Alabama

 ii. JOHN ADAIR was born on 10 Apr 1850 in Alabama. He died on 09 Oct 1852 in Alabama.

   More About John Adair:
   Burial: Salem Cemetery, Salem, Lee County, Alabama

 iii. GEORGE R. ADAIR was born on 28 Jan 1852 in Salem, Alabama. He died on 13 Sep 1853 in Salem, Alabama.

   More About George R. Adair:
   Burial: Salem Cemetery, Salem, Lee County, Alabama

 iv. THOMAS ADAIR was born about 1855 in Alabama.

   More About Thomas Adair:
   Living In: 10 Jul 1860 Living with his father in Smackover Township, Ouachita County, Arkansas.
   Living In: 06 Sep 1860 Living with his uncle, Isaac Ardis, in Pike County, Alabama.

 v. AUGUSTUS ADAIR was born on 14 Jul 1858 in Salem, Alabama. He died on 15 Aug 1858 in Salem, Alabama.

   More About Augustus Adair:
   Burial: Salem Cemetery, Salem, Lee County, Alabama

16. **NEBRASKA KANSAS[4] ARDIS** (John[3], Isaac[2], Mathias[1]) was born on 22 Oct 1857 in Greeneville, Alabama. He died on 18 Feb 1933 in Perdido, Alabama. He married (1) **MARY JANE ODOM**, daughter of Jethro J. Odom and Martha Ellis on 19 Apr 1878 in Greeneville, Butler County, Alabama. She was born on 02 Oct 1860 in Greeneville, Alabama. She died on 28 Feb 1917 in Perdido, Alabama. He married (2) **LILLIE CHAMBLESS**, daughter of David Chambless and Frances M. Avery on 16 Jun 1917 in Perdido, Baldwin County, Alabama. She was born on 31 Dec 1895 in Perdido, Alabama. She died on 22 Apr 1986 in Spanish Fort, Alabama.

More About Nebraska Kansas Ardis:
Burial: 18 Feb 1933 in Perdido Baptist Church Cemetery, Perdido, Alabama
Occupation: 1880 in Starlington, Butler County, Alabama; Farmer

Occupation: 1900 in Fork of Sepulga, Conecuh County, Alabama; Farmer
Occupation: 1910 in Perdido, Baldwin County, Alabama; Farmer
Occupation: 1930 in Perdido, Baldwin County, Alabama; Farmer

Notes for Nebraska Kansas Ardis:
Alabama death index has birth date as November 22, 1858. Headstone has birth date as October 22, 1857.

More About Mary Jane Odom:
Burial: Perdido Baptist Church Cemetery, Perdido, Alabama

Nebraska Kansas Ardis and Mary Jane Odom had the following children:

   i. MARY KANSAS[5] ARDIS was born on 13 Feb 1879 in Starlington, Alabama. She died on 23 Dec 1954. She married William B. Ward on 01 Apr 1906 in Baldwin, Alabama.

33.   ii. JOANNA ARDIS was born on 11 Mar 1882 in Starlington, Butler County, Alabama. She died on 19 Jan 1962 in Austin, Texas. She married Allen Henry Benson, son of William H. Benson and Nancy C. Reid on 01 Apr 1900. He was born on 10 Sep 1879 in Alabama. He died on 26 Jul 1945 in Austin, Texas.

   iii. ETHEL ARIZONA ARDIS was born on 28 Aug 1884 in Starlington, Alabama. She died on 14 Nov 1935 in Mobile, Alabama. She married William Wiley Thomley on 21 Mar 1906 in Baldwin County, Alabama. He was born on 20 Apr 1884. He died on 26 Jun 1967.

      More About Ethel Arizona Ardis:
      Burial: Perdido Baptist Church Cemetery, Perdido, Alabama

34.   iv. JOHNNIE ELIZABETH ARDIS was born on 18 Jan 1887 in Conecuh County, Alabama. She died on 13 Aug 1968 in Mobile, Alabama. She married Louis Claude Havard on 11 Dec 1905. He was born on 30 Jan 1886 in Perdido, Alabama. He died on 11 Apr 1931 in Mobile, Alabama.

   v. LOIS ARDIS was born on 31 Dec 1888 in Conecuh County, Alabama. She died on 23 Nov 1980 in Alabama. She married Luther Virgil Arnette, son of Bob Arnette and Liza Ann Thomley on 18 Dec 1907. He was born on 07 Mar 1885 in Perdido, Alabama. He died on 30 Sep 1938 in Atmore, Escambia County, Alabama.

      More About Lois Ardis:
      Burial: Perdido Baptist Church Cemetery, Perdido, Alabama

   vi. LULA ARDIS was born on 10 Jan 1892 in Conecuh County, Alabama. She died on 18 Jan 1973 in Atmore, Escambia County, Alabama. She married James Edna Dennis on 25 Mar 1909 in Baldwin County, Alabama.

   vii. ROSA LEE ARDIS was born on 08 Feb 1894 in Conecuh County, Alabama. She died on 22 Jul 1974 in Mobile, Mobile County, Alabama. She married (1) POOLEY RUSSELL PATE on 17 Jan 1914. She married CHARLES WOLFSEN.

   viii. NORA MAE ARDIS was born on 19 Nov 1896. She died on 15 Oct 1974. She married George Melvin Harbin on 21 Sep 1929 in Alabama.

ix. LUCY HAZEL ARDIS was born on 30 Jan 1900 in Conecuh County, Alabama. She died on 22 Jan 1967 in Camden, Wilcox County, Alabama. She married John Semon on 11 Aug 1923 in Alabama.

More About Lillie Chambless:
Burial: Mobile Memorial Gardens Cemetery, Tilman's Corner, Mobile County, Alabama
Living In: 1940 Living in Perdido, Baldwin County, Alabama

Nebraska Kansas Ardis and Lillie Chambless had the following children:

35. x. JOHN K. ARDIS was born on 20 Apr 1918 in Perdido, Alabama. He married Vivian Ruth Smith on 24 Sep 1937 in Alabama. She was born about 1918 in Alabama.

xi. HENRY ARDIS was born on 01 Aug 1919 in Perdido, Alabama. He died on 19 Jun 1945. He married Ida Bell Brown on 15 Mar 1938.

xii. EWING CARLISLE ARDIS was born on 07 Sep 1920. He died on 09 Mar 1978. He married CASSIE EDDINS.

xiii. WILLIAM BASCOM ARDIS was born in 1922 in Perdido, Alabama. He married Lillian Mae Davis in 1948.

xiv. CLARENCE ARDIS was born on 12 Feb 1924 in Perdido, Alabama. He married EDITH SIMMONS.

xv. JAMES PATRICK ARDIS was born on 20 Aug 1926 in Perdido, Alabama. He married Cornelius Morris on 08 May 1948.

xvi. VERA MAE ARDIS was born on 02 Jun 1932 in Perdido, Alabama. She married Donald Rolla Schmidt on 23 Sep 1954.

17. **WILLIAM TRAMMELL**[4] **ARDIS** (John[3], Isaac[2], Mathias[1]) was born in Feb 1867 in Greenville, Alabama. He died in 1944 in Escambia County, Florida. He married (1) **SARDELIA WHITTLE** on 24 Apr 1886 in Monroe County, Alabama. She was born in Jul 1864 in Mobile, Alabama. She died in 1926. He married (2) **ELLEN PATE** on 05 Mar 1926 in Brewton County, Alabama. She was born on 01 Jun 1876 in Florida. She died on 15 Dec 1932 in Century, Escambia County, Florida. He married (3) **FLORENCE PEST** on 16 Apr 1933. He married (4) **VERA ARGO** on 01 Apr 1939. She was born about 1903 in Tennessee.

More About William Trammell Ardis:
Burial: Lottie United Methodist Church Cemetery, Lottie, Baldwin County, Alabama Living In: 1935 Escambia County, Florida
Occupation: 1900 in Davis, Van Buren County, Arkansas; Farmer
Occupation: 1920 in Owen, Escambia County, Alabama; Farmer
Occupation: 1930 in Perdido, Butler County, Alabama; Farmer
Occupation: 1940 in Escambia County, Florida; Retired

Notes for William Trammell Ardis:
Headstone gives year of birth as 1868.

More About Sardelia Whittle:
Burial: Lottie United Methodist Church Cemetery, Lottie, Baldwin County, Alabama

William Trammell Ardis and Sardelia Whittle had the following children:

    i.   MARY A.[5] ARDIS was born in Aug 1889 in Alabama.

    ii.   ESTHER ARDIS was born in Oct 1891 in Alabama. She married C.M. Milstead on 23 Feb 1910 in Cause Station, Alabama.

    iii.   MAUD ARDIS was born in Feb 1894 in Alabama.

    iv.   JOHN ARDIS was born in Mar 1896 in Alabama.

    v.   HENRY ARDIS was born in Dec 1897 in Florida.

36.   vi. ISAAC ARDIS was born on 03 Nov 1898 in Mississippi. He died on 03 Feb 1973 in Frisco City, Monroe County, Alabama. He married MAGGIE MARSHALL. She was born on 15 May 1895. She died on 09 Oct 1988.

More About Ellen Pate:
Burial: Springhill Cemetery, Flomaton, Escambia County, Alabama

Notes for Ellen Pate:
Headstone has June 1, 1876 for date of birth. Florida death index has June 1, 1877 for date of birth.

Generation 5

18.   **JOANNA COLUMBIA**[5] **ARDIS** (Isaac[4], John[3], Isaac[2], Mathias[1]) was born on 04 Feb 1847 in Salem, Alabama. She died on 08 Aug 1922 in Greenville, Texas. She married Ambrose Newton Edwards, son of Ambrose Edwards and Emeline James Gaulding on 05 Dec 1865 in Dale County, Alabama. He was born on 21 Oct 1840 in Russell County, Alabama. He died on 20 Jul 1933 in Strawn, Texas.

More About Joanna Columbia Ardis:
Burial: 08 Aug 1922 in Forest Park Cemetery, Greenville, Texas- Moved later to Restland Cemetery, Dallas, Texas
Cause Of Death: Stomach Cancer

Notes for Joanna Columbia Ardis:
Re buried in Restland Cemetery, Dallas, Texas on February 9, 1955, grave marker set on August 31, 1955.

More About Ambrose Newton Edwards:
Burial: 21 Jul 1933 in Forest Park Cemetery, Greenville, Texas- Moved later to Restland Cemetery, Dallas, Texas
Cause Of Death: Prostate Cancer
Occupation: 1860 in Dale County, Alabama; School Teacher
Occupation: 1870 in Sulphur Springs, Texas; Dry Goods Merchant
Occupation: 1880 in Hopkins County, Texas; County Clerk
Occupation: Bet. 27 Mar 1886-20 Oct 1891 ; Postmaster, Eliasville, Texas
Occupation: 1900 in Palo Pinto County, Texas; Lumber Dealer
Occupation: 1910 in Gordon, Palo Pinto County, Texas; Lumber Merchant
Occupation: 1920 in Palo Pinto County, Texas; Retired
Occupation: 1930 in Greenville, Texas; Retired - Living with his son, Ambrose Edwin Edwards
Military Service: Bet. 03 Jul 1861-11 Jun 1865 in C.S.A.; Company E, 15th Alabama Infantry

Notes for Ambrose Newton Edwards:

    Enlisted on July 3, 1861 in Westville, Alabama and served until July 2, 1863 when he was captured at Gettysburg, Pennsylvania and made a prisoner of war. Sent first to Fort McHenry, Maryland on July 5, 1863 and then to Fort Delaware, Delaware on July 6, 1863. Released from Fort Delaware on June 11, 1865.

    Engagements: Winchester, Cross Keys, Harpers Ferry, Sharpsburg, Fredricksburg, Suffolk, Malvern Hill, Cedar Mt. Hazel River, 2nd Manassas, Chantilly, Gettysburg.

    Wounded at Sharpsburg.and Fredricksburg.

    Promoted to Second Sergeant May 15, 1862.
    Promoted to First Sergeant July 25, 1862.
    Promoted to Second Lieutenant but was captured at Gettysburg, Pennsylvania before his commission arrived.

    Pre Civil War Residence was Westville, Alabama.

    Flag of the Army of Northern Virginia covered his casket during his first funeral and burial at Greeneville, Texas.

    Member of the first Board of Regents for the University of Texas 1881-1882

    Buried in Greenville, Texas in 1933 and then buried in Restland Cemetery, Dallas, Texas on February 9, 1955, grave marker set on August 31, 1955.

    Became a Mason at Brightstar Lodge number 221 in Sulphur Springs, Texas on November 5, 1868.

    Death certificate gives October 18, 1840 as date of birth.

Dictated to Emma Irene Garland (Edwards) in 1930

    I well remember the day when my company assembled at old Darian Church in Dale County, Alabama, where we bade good bye to our loved ones and took up our march to the battle front in answer to our country's call.

    I remember the first night we camped on the banks of Pea River and bathed in its waters and spent this our first night in joyous hilarity. I remember after three days march we reached old Fort Mitchell near Columbus Georgia, where we were organized into the 15th Alabama Infantry, my company being known as co. E. Then after a few weeks of company and regimental drill we had orders to go to Virginia, and this was for me a matter of exquisite thrill and interest which cannot be well depicted here.

    When we reached Richmond we were quartered at Old Chimborozo where we remained about three weeks and thence to Manassas. Shortly after the noted first battle of the war, as there was no more fighting in this section, we went into winter quarters there. Up to this time we had not had to suffer any great hardships, but had many interesting experiences.

    In the beginning of 1862, the second year of the war, greater activities in war matters became more tense. McClelland was assembling a great army in the Yorktown peninsula with the purpose of marching on to Richmond and General Johnson was ordered to fall back from Manassas to meet this move of the enemy. But Ewell's division, to which I belonged, was ordered to join Stonewall Jackson in the valley. Then my regiment was in the noted Valley campaign in which Jackson defeated three armies and then it was at Cross Keys we received our baptism of battle. From here the scene changed and the Seven days battle around Richmond was fought in which my regiment took an active part and lost quite a number of noble men.

    I was sick and in the hospital at Charlottesville at that time. After McClelland's defeat General

Lee moved his army North. On the first invasion. we crossed the Potomac at Leesburg, wading it of course as there were no bridges. My division was ordered to go around and cross back above Harper's Ferry where General Wool was stationed with seven thousand men. We had him completely surrounded and he surrendered. In this surrender we secured arms, commissary, and quarter master supplies in great abundance.

Immediately after the surrender we were ordered back across the Potomac to be in the battle of Sharpsburg - called Antietam by the North Historians - this was one of the hardest battles of the war, and was known as a draw. Lee withdrew to the Virginia side and there ended that year's campaign in Virginia.

To avoid being tedious, I will omit many important military operations including the battle of Fredericksburg in which i took a part and will speak of the Pennsylvania invasion and the battle of Gettysburg. I was in this battle and on the second day of July 1863, with thirteen other men of my company was captured and carried to Fort Delaware where we were kept as prisoners until the war closed.

I could make an interesting chapter about our prison, but only say we managed to keep up spirit and hope amid its trials and troubles until the day came for our release nearly two months after the surrender.

I reached home on the 5th of June 1865, to find our beloved Southland wrecked and ruined by war's devastation.

Then it was with unflinching courage we took up the task of reconstructing the ruin and building our new South upon it. While I cannot elaborate on this work, for it would require many words, yet I cannot omit saying that the work was done in a way that solicited the admiration of all people. Our noble women were our staunch co-laborers in every sence, and deserve a monument for their wonderful work.

On the 5th of December 1865 it was my good fortune to lead to the marriage alter one of the best of the noble daughters of the South, to walk with me and share with me, every joy and every sorrow that awaited us on life's pilgrimage. We came to Texas in 1866 where eight sons came to bless our union, all noble men and all living useful lives in Texas except one. Eight years ago my precious one left me to go and wear her crown.

Now in my 90th year I can truly say that much love and kindness have been meted out to me, but must say that the best friends we old veterans have are the noble Daughters of the Confederacy, and may god bless them in my closing word.

> A. N. Edwards
> Co. E. 15th Alabama Inf.

Ambrose Newton Edwards and Joanna Columbia Ardis had the following children:

    i. ISAAC MANSFIELD[6] EDWARDS was born on 01 Feb 1868 in Strawn, Texas. He died on 18 Mar 1945 in Strawn Texas. He married Mary Sophronia (Onie) Strawn, daughter of Stephen Bethel Strawn and Emeline Jane Allen in 1899 in Palo Pinto County, Texas. She was born on 11 Apr 1874 in Strawn, Texas. She died on 18 Feb 1950 in Temple, Bell County, Texas.

More About Isaac Mansfield Edwards:
Burial: 19 Mar 1945 in Mount Marion Cemetery, Strawn, Texas
Cause Of Death: Coronary Thrombosis and Embolism
Occupation: 1900 in Palo Pinto County, Texas; Farmer
Occupation: 1910 in Strawn, Texas; Carpenter
Occupation: 1920 in Weatherford, Texas; Carpenter

Occupation: 1930 in Strawn, Texas; Painter
Occupation: 1940 in Strawn, Texas; Painter

Notes for Isaac Mansfield Edwards:
Death certificate gives date of birth as February 1, 1868. 1900 U.S. census gives
date of birth as February 1868. Headstone gives date of birth as February 1, 1870.

ii.   WALTER WHITE EDWARDS was born on 31 Oct 1870 in Sulphur Springs, Texas. He
died on 27 Nov 1938 in El Paso, Texas. He married Mary Anna King, daughter
of Porter King and Eudorah Martha Bush in 1897 in Palo Pinto County, Texas.
She was born on 23 Jul 1864 in Texas. She died on 23 Dec 1956 in Amarillo,
Potter County, Texas.

More About Walter White Edwards:
Burial: 29 Nov 1938 in Evergreen Cemetery, El Paso,
Texas
Cause Of Death: Cardiac Failure, Hypertension
Occupation: 1910; Gold Miner, Gorden, Palo Pinto County,
Texas
Occupation: 1920; Salesman, El Paso, Texas
Occupation: 193 ; Geologist, El Paso, Texas

Notes for Walter White
    Edwards: Dear Mr. Edwards:
    Your request to our Geological Information Center for information on the
Baking Powder mine was forwarded to me. Probably fewer than a half-dozen
living people in all the southwest have even heard of
this property as it is one of the more obscure such in all New Mexico. I am not
aware that the property was ever examined by a trained geologist or engineer
(unless your Edwards relatives were such and there is no known surviving record
of their work). My extensive mines and prospects files are absolutely silent in
regard to the Baking Powder. Nevertheless I have noted one or two very obscure
references in my research.
    The Baking Powder is located in the Rosedale Mining District at the extreme
north end of the San Mateo mountains in southern Socorro county, New Mexico. I
have not examined the mining claim records in the local courthouse for exact
dates (mainly because you are the very first individual to ever request information
on the property!) but would predict the claim (or claims) was located during latter
part of the 19th century -- poss. mid-1890s -- as a result of the success of the
well-known Rosedale mine and discovery of the nearby White Cap.
    The "veins" in the Rosedale district are actually brecciated shear zones in the
volcanic (rhyolitic) rocks The brecciated and sheared rhyolite has been recemented
with a hard, bluish-white quartz and later with a clearer vein-type quartz. The entire
vein mass is highly silicified and in those areas yielding the best gold values are
heavily stained with the black and red oxides of manganese and iron respectively. Gold
occurred in the native state in the upper oxidized portions of the vein but is very nearly
absent in the sulfide portion at or below the water table. Remarkably, little or no silver
is present. I would predict the Baking Powder "vein" to be similar in character to the
above. Dr. Charles Ferguson's doctoral dissertation covered a large area extending
from the southern end of the Rosedale District to the north well beyond White Cap and
Big Rosa canyons. I asked Charlie if he knew the locality of the Baking Powder and
other prospects and he indicated approximate locations for two unnamed mine
workings about two miles north and northwest of the Rosedale which I feel are the
White Cap and the Baking Powder. The projected location for the latter is approx.
Sec3, T6S, R6W near the head of Big Rosa canyon.
    Soon after the turn of the century, development on the Baking Powder had

apparently progressed to the mining stage. According to a note in the Engineering and Mining Journal, 24 December 1903, p 988, the Baking Powder mine was said to be initiating "full operations," whatever that meant; Walter Edwards, undoubtedly your ancestor, was the manager. Unfortunately the operation failed to live up to expectations and within four years was facing foreclosure for $1200 in back wages (Soccoro Chieftan, 30 November 1907). The obvious conclusion is that the mine failed to develop pay ore in sufficient quantities to sustain the operation and it failed. And that is the current extent of the "historic" record!

I and my colleagues attempted to visit this prospect in May 2000, but despite our "approximate" location on the topo sheet, and a full day's search, four-wheeling, etc., we failed to locate it. I should note that the 'road' up Big Rosa canyon is, in places, a figment of the imagination -- we could have easily missed a small prospect off in the ponderosas! The Mount Whithington jeep road may pass within a mile of the mine on the west and that is the route I will next attempt.

Now that you have made a request for information, I shall keep a sharp lookout for additional data. I must yet peruse the pages of the few issues of the San Marcial Bee that have survived the ravages of time and will keep you in mind should anything materialize. Additionally I will examine the claim location records upon my next visit to the courthouse. On the other hand, I'd be most pleased to add to our archival files any information you'd be willing to share with us from your family's papers. Regards,

Robert W. Eveleth Senior
Mining Engineer Curator,
Mining Archives

Dear Mr. Edwards:

Recent research on several articles of local mining interest has, once again, led me through the pages of the Socorro Chieftain. Recalling your interest in the above, I made a copy of an article on the Baking Powder/Edwards Bros., reproduced below in its entirety:

Socorro Chieftain, 6/14/1902, p 4: "Rosedale, N. M., June 10m, 1902 -- Editor Chieftain -- Rosedale is quiet at present. Big Rosa, 2-1/2 miles to the northwest, shows great and rapidly increasing activity. Fully $5,000 worth of work is now underway and other contracts are being let. The immediate cause of this work was the discovery and partial development of the Baking Powder property of the Edwards Brothers of El Paso, Tex. This claim showed well from the surface but now at a depth of 55 feet it is exciting old time prospectors and tenderfeet alike by yielding a strong vein of high grade ore while picked samples show as high as 84 ounces in gold. Two or more stamp mills, stores, drink emporiums, a post office, dozens of cabins and tents, a good graded road up Big Rosa, and a couple of hundred men tearing into its mountain sides may be a vision, but as a miner and prospector of long experience I think this and more will be a reality within 12 months. Big Rosa may not be as good a mining camp as Cripple Creek, Colo. It may be better. The writer has no interest there and is not puffing the camp to "induce capital," but is sincere in saying that right now is a suitable and very favorable time to investigate Big Rosa.
There can be no harm in keeping an eye on the indicator." Signed: A. L. Heister."

As I continue to go through the pages of the Socorro Chieftan, I'll be sure to let you know if the writer's dream materialized.

Best Regards,
Robert W. Eveleth
Senior Mining Engineer

----

iii.   AMBROSE EDWIN EDWARDS was born on 20 Mar 1872 in Sulphur Springs, Texas. He died on 15 Feb 1963 in Dallas, Texas. He married Anne Buntin Yarbrough, daughter of George Yarbrough and Margaret Augusta Herrin on 03 Jul 1901 in Grayson County, Texas. She was born on 15 Oct 1871 in Tyler, Texas. She died on 24 Oct 1955 in Dallas, Texas.

More About Ambrose Edwin Edwards:
Burial: 18 Feb 1963 in Restland Cemetery, Dallas, Texas
Cause Of Death: Cerebral Arteriosclerosis
Occupation: 1910 in Greenville, Texas; Real Estate Agent
Occupation: 1920 in Greenville, Texas; Real Estate Agent
Occupation: 1930 in Greenville, Texas; Farm Loan Agent
Occupation: 1940 in Dallas, Texas; Real Estate Proprietor

Notes for Ambrose Edwin Edwards:
Middle name of Edwin is probably after Doctor Edwin P. Becton of Sulphur Springs, Texas.

  Birth date is from Social Security death index. Headstone has 1871 for year of birth but this would conflict with the birth date of his brother, Walter White Edwards.

iv.   MARVIN M. EDWARDS was born on 28 Nov 1875 in Riley Springs, Texas. He died on 11 Sep 1900 in Strawn, Texas.

More About Marvin M. Edwards:
Burial: Mount Marion Cemetery, Strawn, Texas
Cause Of Death: Consumption (Tuberculosis)
Living In: 1900 Palo Pinto County, Texas with his parents

v.   MCDONALD EDWARDS was born on 10 Dec 1877 in Strawn, Texas. He died on 08 Nov 1957 in Lubbock, Texas. He married Sally May Marchbanks, daughter of Finley W. Marchbanks and Sarah A. Hix on 26 Feb 1899 in Strawn, Texas. She was born on 12 Feb 1877 in Cleburne, Texas. She died on 27 Oct 1957 in Fort Worth, Texas.

More About McDonald Edwards:
Burial: 08 Nov 1957 in O'Donnell Cemetery, O'Donnell, Texas
Cause Of Death: Nephrosclerosis
Occupation: 1900 in Palo Pinto County, Texas; Hack Man
Occupation: 1910 in Palo Pinto County, Texas; Lumber Merchant
Occupation: 1920 in Palo Pinto County, Texas; Lumber Merchant
Occupation: 1930 in O'Donnell, Texas; Lumber Yard Manager
Occupation: 1940 in O'Donnell, Texas; Lumber Yard Proprietor

vi.   LEROY ARDIS EDWARDS was born on 27 Feb 1881 in Sulphur Springs, Texas. He died on 05 Dec 1951 in Loraine, Texas. He married (1) EMMA GEORGIE IRENE GARLAND, daughter of Edward Warren Garland and Julia Rebecca Kimbell on 27 Jul 1921 in Roscoe, Texas. She was born on 23 Mar 1880 in Annona, Texas. She died on 17 Dec 1969 in Kerrville, Texas. He married (2) ADA MAY LOFLIN, daughter of Daniel Vance Loflin and Margarite Sophia Crawley on 21 Nov 1906 in Palo Pinto

County, Texas. She was born on 26 Apr 1886 in Palo Pinto County, Texas.
She died on 15 Apr 1918 in Loraine, Texas.

More About LeRoy Ardis Edwards:
Burial: 07 Dec 1951 in Loraine Cemetery, Loraine,
Texas Cause Of Death: Carcinoma of Lung
Occupation: 1910 in Brazoria County, Texas; Truck Farmer
Occupation: 1918 in Ranger, Eastland County, Texas; Manager of Buell
Lumber Company
Occupation: 1920 in Loraine, Texas; Lumber Yard Manager
Occupation: 1930 in Loraine, Texas; Lumber Yard Manager
Occupation: 1940 in Olton, Texas; Retail Lumber Yard Manager
Occupation: 1942 in Olton, Lamb County, Texas; Manager of
Higgingbotham Lumber Company

Notes for LeRoy Ardis Edwards:

Discovered and operated, with his brother Walter, "Baking Powder" gold
mine near Rosedale, New Mexico.

Dear Mr. Edwards:

Your request to our Geological Information Center for information on the
Baking Powder mine was forwarded to me. Probably fewer than a half-dozen
living people in all the southwest have even heard of
this property as it is one of the more obscure such in all New Mexico. I am not
aware that the property was ever examined by a trained geologist or engineer
(unless your Edwards relatives were such and there is no known surviving record
of their work). My extensive mines and prospects files are absolutely silent in
regard to the Baking Powder. Nevertheless I have noted one or two very obscure
references in my research.

The Baking Powder is located in the Rosedale Mining District at the extreme north
end of the San Mateo mountains in southern Socorro county, New Mexico. I have not
examined the mining claim records in the local courthouse for exact dates (mainly
because you are the very first individual to ever request information on the property!)
but would predict the claim (or claims) was located during latter part of
the 19th century -- poss. mid-1890s -- as a result of the success of the well-known
Rosedale mine and discovery of the nearby White Cap.

The "veins" in the Rosedale district are actually brecciated shear zones in the
volcanic (rhyolitic) rocks The brecciated and sheared rhyolite has been recemented
with a hard, bluish-white quartz and later with a clearer vein-type quartz. The entire
vein mass is highly silicified and in those areas yielding the best gold values are
heavily stained with the black and red oxides of manganese and iron respectively. Gold
occurred in the native state in the upper oxidized portions of the vein but is very nearly
absent in the sulfide portion at or below the water table. Remarkably, little or no silver
is present. I would predict the Baking Powder "vein" to be similar in character to the
above. Dr. Charles Ferguson's doctoral dissertation covered a large area extending
from the southern end of the Rosedale District to the north well beyond White Cap and
Big Rosa canyons. I asked Charlie if he knew the locality of the Baking Powder and
other prospects and he indicated approximate locations for two unnamed mine
workings about two miles north and northwest of the Rosedale

which I feel are the White Cap and the Baking Powder. The projected location for the latter is approx. Sec3, T6S, R6W near the head of Big Rosa canyon.

Soon after the turn of the century, development on the Baking Powder had apparently progressed to the mining stage. According to a note in the Engineering and Mining Journal, 24 December 1903, p 988, the Baking Powder mine was said to be initiating "full operations," whatever that meant; Walter Edwards, undoubtedly your ancestor, was the manager. Unfortunately the operation failed to live up to expectations and within four years was facing foreclosure for $1200 in back wages (Soccoro Chieftan, 30 November 1907). The obvious conclusion is that the mine failed to develop pay ore in sufficient quantities to sustain the operation and it failed. And that is the current extent of the "historic" record!

I and my colleagues attempted to visit this prospect in May 2000, but despite our "approximate" location on the topo sheet, and a full day's search, four-wheeling, etc., we failed to locate it. I should note that the 'road' up Big Rosa canyon is, in places, a figment of the imagination -- we could have easily missed a small prospect off in the ponderosas! The Mount Whithington jeep road may pass within a mile of the mine on the west and that is the route I will next attempt.

Now that you have made a request for information, I shall keep a sharp lookout for additional data. I must yet peruse the pages of the few issues of the San Marcial Bee that have survived the ravages of time and will keep you in mind should anything materialize. Additionally I will examine the claim location records upon my next visit to the courthouse. On the other hand, I'd be most pleased to add to our archival files any information you'd be willing to share with us from your family's papers. Regards,
Robert W. Eveleth Senior
Mining Engineer Curator,
Mining Archives

Dear Mr. Edwards:

Recent research on several articles of local mining interest has, once again, led me through the pages of the Socorro Chieftain. Recalling your interest in the above, I made a copy of an article on the Baking Powder/Edwards Bros., reproduced below in its entirety:

Socorro Chieftain, 6/14/1902, p 4: "Rosedale, N. M., June 10m, 1902 -- Editor Chieftain -- Rosedale is quiet at present. Big Rosa, 2-1/2 miles to the northwest, shows great and rapidly increasing activity. Fully $5,000 worth of work is now underway and other contracts are being let. The immediate cause of this work was the discovery and partial development of the Baking Powder property of the Edwards Brothers of El Paso, Tex. This claim showed well from the surface but now at a depth of 55 feet it is exciting old time prospectors and tenderfeet alike by yielding a strong vein of high grade ore while picked samples show as high as 84 ounces in gold. Two or more stamp mills, stores, drink emporiums, a post office, dozens of cabins and tents, a good graded road up Big Rosa, and a couple of hundred men tearing into its mountain sides may be a vision, but as a miner and prospector of long experience I think this and more will be a reality within 12 months. Big Rosa may not be as good a mining camp as Cripple Creek, Colo. It may be better. The writer has no interest there and is not puffing the camp to "induce capital," but is sincere in saying that right now is a suitable and very favorable time to investigate Big Rosa.
There can be no harm in keeping an eye on the indicator." Signed: A. L. Heister."

As I continue to go through the pages of the Socorro Chieftan, I'll be sure to let you know if the writer's dream materialized.

Best Regards,
Robert W. Eveleth
Senior Mining Engineer

----

vii.   BECTON GOODSON EDWARDS was born on 29 Oct 1884 in Sulphur Springs, Texas. He died on 04 Dec 1960 in Dallas, Dallas County, Texas. He married Minnie Mae Strain, daughter of George Douglas Strain and Sarah Elizabeth Strawn on 04 Nov 1908 in Weatherford, Texas. She was born on 22 Feb 1887 in Strawn, Texas. She died on 28 Jul 1956 in Corsicana, Navarro County, Texas.

More About Becton Goodson Edwards:
Burial: 06 Dec 1960 in Grove Hill Cemetery, Dallas, Dallas County, Texas
Cause Of Death: Coronary Occlusion, Arteriosclerosis Heart Valve
Occupation: 1910 in Weatherford, Texas; Real Estate and Insurance Salesman
Occupation: 1920 in Forney, Texas; Postmaster
Occupation: 1930 in Forney, Texas; Pharmacist
Occupation: 1940 in Forney, Texas; Retail Drug Store Manager

Notes for Becton Goodson Edwards:
Named after Doctor Edwin P. Becton of Sulphur Springs, Texas. Doctor Becton served in the 22nd Texas Infantry, C.S.A., during the Civil War and is buried in Sulphur Springs City Cemetery, Sulphur Springs, Texas.
----

viii. JOHN MCTYEIRE EDWARDS was born on 08 Dec 1888 in Eliasville, Texas. He died on 05 Oct 1970 in Killeen, Texas.

More About John McTyeire Edwards:
Burial: 09 Oct 1970 in Fort Sam Houston National Cemetery, San Antonio, Texas Cause Of Death: Acute Myocardio Infarction, Generalized Arteriosclerosis
Living In: 1910 Greenville, Texas
Occupation: 1920 in Palo Pinto County, Texas; Bank Cashier
Occupation: 1930 in San Antonio, Texas; Hotel Clerk
Occupation: 1940 in San Antonio, Texas; Private Residence Gardener
Military Service: Bet. 19 Sep 1917-24 Mar 1919; Sergeant First Class, World War One

Notes for John McTyeire
Edwards: Never Married

Probably named after John McTyeire of Russell County, Alabama.

Served in HQ Company, 165th Depot Brigade, U.S. Army
----

19.   **JOHNATHAN WHITE[5] ARDIS** (Isaac[4], John[3], Isaac[2], Mathias[1]) was born in Apr 1850 in Salem, Alabama. He died on 11 May 1917 in San Antonio, Bexar County, Texas. He married Rosa Lee Brinker on 21 Nov 1875 in Sulphur Springs, Texas. She was born in Apr 1853 in Shelby County,

Alabama. She died on 27 Jun 1919 in Sulphur Springs, Hopkins County, Texas.

More About Johnathan White Ardis:
Burial: City Cemetery, Sulphur Springs, Texas
Cause Of Death: Chronic Nephritis and Arteriosclerosis
Occupation: 1870 in Hopkins County, Texas; Working on farm.
Occupation: 1880 in Hopkins County, Texas; Farmer
Occupation: 1900 in Sulphur Springs, Hopkins County, Texas; Cotton Buyer
Occupation: 1910 in Sulphur Springs, Hopkins County, Texas; Cotton Buyer

More About Rosa Lee Brinker:
Burial: 30 Jun 1919 in City Cemetery, Sulphur Springs, Hopkins County,
Texas
Cause Of Death: Dysentery

Notes for Rosa Lee Brinker:
Ardis, White, Mrs. - died last Sunday after a lingering illness and remains were buried in the City
Cemetery, with funeral services being conducted by Pastor Mood of the First Methodist Church
of which the deceased had been a long devout member. She was buried beside her husband
who died May 1917. She was 65 years old, having been born in Alabama in 1854, and lived in
Hopkins County for the past 45 years. In 1875, she was married to J.W. Ardis. To this union
were born three children as follows: Mrs. J. Manly Carter of Chickasha, OK, Louis Ardis of
Sulphur Springs, and Dollie Ardis who died early in Life. (Hopkins Co. Echo, July 4, 1919).

Johnathan White Ardis and Rosa Lee Brinker had the following children:

     i.   DOLLIE[6] ARDIS was born in 1878 in Sulphur Springs, Texas. She died on 15
            Apr 1887 in Sulphur Springs, Texas.

    ii.   LEWIS H. ARDIS was born on 09 Nov 1881 in Sulphur Springs, Texas. He died on
            14 Feb 1931 in Sulphur Springs, Hopkins County, Texas.

            More About Lewis H. Ardis:
            Burial: 14 Feb 1931 in City Cemetery, Sulphur Springs,
            Texas
            Cause Of Death: Rheumatism
            Living In: 1910 Living with his parents in Sulphur Springs, Texas.
            Occupation: 1900 in Sulphur Springs, Hopkins County, Texas; Farm Hand
            Occupation: 1910 in Sulphur Springs, Hopkins County, Texas; Cotton Buyer
            Occupation: 1931 in Sulphur Springs, Hopkins County, Texas; Grocery Merchant

            Notes for Lewis H. Ardis:
            "Lewis Ardis passed away Saturday after a short illness. He was a splendid
            business man in this town where he was born and spent his entire life. He was
            49 years old and is survived by his wife and one sister, Mrs. J. M. Carter of
            Oklahoma City. Funeral services were held at Myra Wilson Chapel and burial in
            the City Cemetery. (Daily News-Telegram, Feb 1931)."

            Headstone has November 9, 1882 for date of birth. Obituary and death
            certificate indicate November 9, 1881 is date of birth.

20.   ISAAC[5] ARDIS (Isaac[4], John[3], Isaac[2], Mathias[1]) was born on 16 Dec 1851 in Salem, Alabama. He
       died on 13 Apr 1913 in Greenville, Texas. He married Martha J. Taylor, daughter of Alexander Taylor
       and Margaret Davis on 05 Dec 1875 in Hunt County, Texas. She was born on 18 Oct 1843

in Marshall County, Tennessee. She died on 07 Feb 1923 in Greenville, Texas.

More About Isaac Ardis:
Burial: 13 Apr 1913 in East Mount Cemetery, Greenville, Texas
Occupation: 1870 in Hopkins County, Texas; Working on farm.
Occupation: 1880 in Hunt County, Texas; Doctor
Occupation: 1900 in Hunt County, Texas; Druggist
Occupation: 1910 in Hunt County, Texas; Medical Practitioner

Notes for Isaac Ardis:
Headstone has December 16, 1851 for date of birth. Death certificate has December 16, 1850 for date of birth.

Listed in Directory of Deceased American Physicians.

More About Martha J. Taylor:
Burial: 08 Feb 1923 in East Mount Cemetery, Greenville, Texas
Cause Of Death: Arterioschlerosis

Isaac Ardis and Martha J. Taylor had the following children:

    i.   JOSEPHINE[6] ARDIS was born on 17 Feb 1877 in Greenville, Texas. She died on 16 Nov 1955 in Greenville, Texas. She married George Lawrence Rutherford, son of James W. Rutherford and Martha Louisa Hynson on 18 Dec 1901 in Hunt County, Texas. He was born on 27 Jan 1867 in Arkansas. He died on 25 Oct 1929 in Dallas, Texas.

         More About Josephine Ardis:
         Burial: 17 Nov 1955 in East Mount Cemetery, Greenville, Texas
         Cause Of Death: ; Cerebral Hemorrhage
         Living In: 1900 Living with her parents in Hunt County, Texas.
         Occupation: 1897; School Teacher, Eliasville, Texas
         Occupation: 1900 in Hunt County, Texas; School Teacher

    ii.   RUSH ISAAC ARDIS was born on 15 Sep 1878 in Greenville, Texas. He died on 02 Oct 1949 in Greenville, Texas. He married Myrtle Mae McGaughey on 22 Nov 1905 in Hunt County, Texas. She was born on 22 Jul 1885. She died on 08 May 1981 in Dallas County, Texas.

         More About Rush Isaac Ardis:
         Burial: 04 Oct 1949 in East Mount Cemetery, Greenville, Texas
         Cause Of Death: Congestive Heart Failure
         Living In: 1900 Living with his parents in Hunt County, Texas
         Living In: 1942 Greenville, Texas
         Occupation: Merchant

    iii.   HORACE ARDIS was born on 04 Sep 1880 in Greenville, Texas. He died on 17 Jun 1936 in Hunt County, Texas. He married Bertha Moore, daughter of Atlas B. Moore and Jessie Shaw on 23 Apr 1902 in Hunt County, Texas. She was born on 29 Jul 1880 in Tennessee. She died on 07 Sep 1953 in Terrell, Texas.

More About Horace Ardis:
Burial: 19 Jun 1936 in East Mount Cemetery, Greenville, Texas
Cause Of Death: Coronary Disease and accidental blow to back of neck.

iv.　JENNIE KATE ARDIS was born on 20 Dec 1881 in Greenville, Texas. She died on 21 Aug 1953 in Houston, Texas. She married WILLIAM GAFFORD. She married JAMES A. PHILLIPS.

More About Jennie Kate Ardis:
Burial: Greenville, Texas
Cause Of Death: Cerebral Hemorrhage

Notes for Jennie Kate Ardis:
Death certificate gives first name as Katherine.
Death certificate gives birth date as August 20, 1880. 1900 U. S. census gives month and year of birth as December 1882.

21.　**ROBERT HENRY[5] ARDIS** (Isaac[4], John[3], Isaac[2], Mathias[1]) was born on 21 Jan 1854 in Salem, Alabama. He died on 17 Dec 1932 in Eliasville, Texas. He married Amanda A. Wells, daughter of William Wells and (unknown) Carver on 27 Dec 1877 in Sulphur Springs, Texas. She was born on 11 Mar 1859 in Sulphur Springs, Texas. She died on 26 Oct 1926 in Eliasville, Texas.

More About Robert Henry Ardis:
Burial: 18 Dec 1932 in Eliasville Cemetery, Eliasville, Texas
Occupation: 1880 in Hopkins County, Texas; Farmer
Occupation: 1900 in Throckmorton County, Texas; Farmer
Occupation: 1910 in Young County, Texas; Farmer
Occupation: 1920 in Young County, Texas; Farmer
Occupation: 1930 in Young County, Texas; Retired

More About Amanda A. Wells:
Burial: 28 Oct 1926 in Eliasville Cemetery, Eliasville, Texas
Cause Of Death: Apoplexy

Robert Henry Ardis and Amanda A. Wells had the following children:

i.　LESTER A.[6] ARDIS was born in Mar 1881 in Sulphur Springs, Texas. He married EMMA BOYD.

ii.　EULA ARDIS was born on 19 Jul 1883 in Sulphur Springs, Texas. She died on 18 Dec 1958 in Wichita Falls, Texas. She married JOHN W. PARROTT.

More About Eula Ardis:
Burial: 18 Dec 1958 in Graham Cemetery, Graham, Texas Cause Of Death: Acute Necrotizing Pancreatitis

iii.　WILLIAM HOWARD ARDIS was born on 07 May 1886 in Eliasville, Texas. He died on 24 May 1908 in Eliasville, Texas. He married IDA JANE YANCEY. She was born on 22 Dec 1885 in Texas. She died on 14 Jul 1937 in Fort Worth, Texas.

More About William Howard Ardis:
Burial: Eliasville Cemetery, Eliasville, Texas

iv.   MODENA ARDIS was born on 07 Dec 1888 in Eliasville, Texas. She died on 03 Sep 1970 in Graham, Young County, Texas. She married H. Edgar Davis on 03 May 1912 in Young County, Texas. He died before 03 Sep 1970.

More About Modena Ardis:
Burial: 05 Sep 1970 in Eliasville Cemetery, Eliasville, Texas
Cause Of Death: Coronary Occlusion
Living In: 1910 Living with her parents in Young County, Texas.
Occupation: 1910 in Young County, Texas; School Teacher

v.   FLORA ARDIS was born on 07 Jun 1891 in Eliasville, Texas. She died on 10 Mar 1976 in Graham, Texas. She married (1) ROY MCCHAREN, son of Edward McCharen and Elizabeth Zenobia Jerrigan on 01 Sep 1912 in Eliasville, Young County, Texas. He was born on 17 Apr 1891 in Toccopola, Pontotoc county, Mississippi. He died on 16 Jul 1943 in Eliasville, Texas. She married (UNKNOWN) ARNOLD.

More About Flora Ardis:
Burial: Eliasville Cemetery, Eliasville, Texas

vi.   ALLYE ARDIS was born in Feb 1894 in Eliasville, Texas. She died in 1983 in Young County, Texas. She married Greene E. Newell, son of D. J. Newell and Henrietta Alexander on 30 Dec 1919 in Eliasville, Texas. He was born on 29 Oct 1882 in Mississippi. He died on 24 Oct 1948 in Borger, Texas.

More About Allye Ardis:
Burial: Eliasville Cemetery, Eliasville, Texas

vii.   CHARLIE C. ARDIS was born on 04 Feb 1897 in Eliasville, Texas. He died on 09 Dec 1965 in Borger, Texas. He married JUANITA DAVIS. She was born in 1907. She died in 1991.

More About Charlie C. Ardis:
Burial: 10 Dec 1965 in Eliasville Cemetery, Eliasville, Texas
Cause Of Death: Cardiac Arrest
Living In: 1920 Living with his parents in Young County, Texas
Living In: 1930 Living with his father in Young County, Texas
Occupation: 1920 in Young County, Texas; Oil Field Laborer
Occupation: 1930 in Young County, Texas; School Bus Driver for Public School
Occupation: Retail Clothing
Military Service: World War One

22.   **WILLIAM HOWARD**[5] **ARDIS** (Isaac[4], John[3], Isaac[2], Mathias[1]) was born on 23 Apr 1856 in Pike County, Alabama. He died on 18 Sep 1924 in Eliasville, Texas. He married Edna Earl Collins, daughter of Henry Clay Collins and Mary Ann Darwin in 1885 in Greenville, Hopkins County, Texas. She was born on 07 Apr 1868 in Tennessee. She died on 09 Jan 1907 in Eliasville, Texas.

More About William Howard Ardis:
Burial: Oak Grove Cemetery, Graham, Texas
Living In: 1900 Young County, Texas
Occupation: 1880 in Hopkins County, Texas; Working on his mother's
farm
Occupation: Bet. 20 Oct 1891-22 Jun 1894 ; Postmaster, Eliasville,
Texas
Occupation: 1900 in Young County, Texas; General Merchant
Occupation: 1910 in Young County, Texas; Farmer
Occupation: 1920 in Terry County, Texas; Farmer

More About Edna Earl Collins:
Burial: Oak Grove Cemetery, Graham, Texas

William Howard Ardis and Edna Earl Collins had the following children:

    i.   WILLIE E.[6] ARDIS was born on 14 Aug 1886 in Eliasville, Texas. She died on 08 Feb 1967 in San Antonio, Texas. She married James A. Gore on 22 Jul 1906 in Young County, Texas. He was born on 12 Jan 1885 in Texas. He died on 09 Oct 1970 in San Antonio, Twxas.

       More About Willie E. Ardis:
       Burial: 11 Feb 1967 in San Jose Burial Park, San Antonio,
       Texas Cause Of Death: ; Myocardial Infarction

    ii.   ISAAC HENRY ARDIS was born on 17 Jan 1889 in Eliasville, Texas. He died on 02 Mar 1957 in Odessa, Texas. He married Maggie Bell Price, daughter of Joseph Price on 01 Nov 1911 in Young County, Texas. She was born in 1886 in Texas. She died in 1966.

       More About Isaac Henry Ardis:
       Burial: 05 Mar 1957 in Sunset Memorial Gardens, Odessa,
       Texas
       Cause Of Death: Coronary Occlusion
       Living In: 1919   Crystal Falls, Texas
       Living In: 1942 South Bend, Texas
       Occupation: Worked for Phillips Petroleum Company

       Notes for Isaac Henry Ardis:
       Death certificate gives date of birth as January 17, 1889. 1900 U.S. census gives month and year of birth as June 1889.

    iii.   DORA KATE ARDIS was born on 09 Jun 1891 in Eliasville, Texas. She died on 25 Nov 1970 in Tulia, Texas. She married Thomas A. Fletcher on 03 Sep 1911 in Young County, Texas.

       More About Dora Kate Ardis:
       Burial: 27 Nov 1970 in Rose Hill Cemetery, Tulia,
       Texas Cause Of Death: Myocardial Infarction

    iv.   BESSIE M. ARDIS was born on 09 Jan 1894 in Eliasville, Texas. She died on 25 Nov 1978 in Pampa, Gray County, Texas. She married Robert L. Souter on 03 Jun 1911 in Young County, Texas. He died before 25 Nov 1978.

       More About Bessie M. Ardis:
       Burial: 27 Nov 1978 in Fairview Cemetery, Pampa, Texas

Cause Of Death: Congestive Heart Failure

     v.   JOHN BRYAN ARDIS was born in Jul 1896 in Eliasville, Texas.

           Notes for John Bryan Ardis:
           Died in World War One.

     vi.   LOIS N. ARDIS was born in Jan 1899 in Eliasville, Texas. She married CHARLES HOAG.

     vii.   ONNIE C. ARDIS was born in 1902 in Eliasville, Texas. She married CLAUDE PEELER.

     viii. ROBERT EDWARD LEE ARDIS was born on 14 Jul 1903 in Eliasville, Texas. He died on 22 Oct 1956 in Tulia, Texas. He married CLARA MAY MUDD. She was born on 25 Sep 1907. She died on 05 Dec 1930 in Tulia, Texas. He married (2) MAY ARMONTROUT WHITE in 1932.

           More About Robert Edward Lee Ardis:
           Burial: 23 Oct 1956 in Rose Hill Cemetery, Tulia, Texas
           Cause Of Death: Pneumonia following Ulcer Surgery
           Occupation: 1956 in Tulia, Texas; Farmer

     ix.   MATTIE EARL BERTRUDE ARDIS was born on 09 Aug 1907 in Eliasville, Texas. She died on 27 Aug 1938 in Snyder, Texas. She married (1) MILTON MASON SMITH in 1919 in Eliasville, Texas. She married OLIVER BRADLEY BURGESS. He was born in 1900. He died in 1974.

           More About Mattie Earl Bertrude Ardis:
           Burial: 28 Aug 1938 in Ira Cemetery, Ira, Scurry County, Texas
           Cause Of Death: Toxemia from Acute Appendix.

           Notes for Mattie Earl Bertrude Ardis:
           Death certificate gives birth date as November 20, 1905. Headstone gives birth year as 1907.

23.   **JAMES E.**[5] **ARDIS** (Isaac[4], John[3], Isaac[2], Mathias[1]) was born on 09 Jul 1861 in Westville, Alabama. He died on 24 Sep 1934 in Sulphur Springs, Texas. He married Clistia Ellen Chapin, daughter of Paul Stilman Chapin and Matilda (unknown) on 22 Aug 1883 in Sulphur Springs, Texas. She was born on 22 Aug 1866 in Sulphur Springs, Texas. She died on 24 Mar 1934 in Sulphur Springs, Texas.

More About James E. Ardis:
Burial: 25 Sep 1934 in Gafford Chapel Cemetery, Hopkins County, Texas
Cause Of Death: Peritonitis
Occupation: 1880 in Hopkins County, Texas; Farming with his mother.
Occupation: 1900 in Hopkins County, Texas; Farmer
Occupation: 1920 in Sulphur Springs, Hopkins County, Texas; Farmer
Occupation: 1930 in Hopkins County, Texas; Farmer

Notes for James E. Ardis:

Ardis, J. E. -1861 -1934 (Obituary)
    J. E. Ardis, age 73, passed away Monday afternoon, Sept. 24, 1934, at the home of his daughter, Mrs. Dowe Harris, at Overland, following a stroke Saturday night. His wife passed away exactly six months ago. He is survived by two daughters, Mrs. Nonnie Russell, Commerce, and Mrs. Vergoe Harris, Overland; one son, Julius Ardis, of Gafford Chapel, and one brother, Julius, of California. One daughter, Miss Omar (sic) Ardis, passed away seven years ago. Funeral services and burial were held at Gafford's Chapel, conducted by Dr. J. Sam Barcus. He was a native of Kentucky and came to Texas with his father's family early in life and settled in Gafford's Chapel community where he has lived over half a century. (Hopkins Co. Echo, Sept. 28, 1934)
    (NOTE: James E. Ardis was from Alabama not Kentucky.)

More About Clistia Ellen Chapin:
Burial: 24 Mar 1934 in Gafford Chapel Cemetery, Hopkins County, Texas
Cause Of Death: Heart Failure

Notes for Clistia Ellen Chapin:
Headstone has 1867 for year of birth. Death certificate has August 22, 1866 for date of birth.

James E. Ardis and Clistia Ellen Chapin had the following children:

i.   NONNIE[6] ARDIS was born on 25 Oct 1884 in Sulphur Springs, Texas. She died on 12 Aug 1943 in Sulphur Springs, Texas. She married JODIE RUSSELL. He was born on 01 Sep 1885 in Texas. He died on 24 Mar 1976 in Hunt County, Texas.

      More About Nonnie Ardis:
      Burial: Gafford Chapel Cemetery, Hopkins County, Texas

ii.   JULIUS LEONARD ARDIS was born on 12 Jul 1889 in Sulphur Springs, Texas. He died on 31 May 1964 in Sulphur Springs, Texas. He married Martha Ellen Taylor, daughter of Erastus W. Taylor and Sallie E. (unknown) on 14 Sep 1913 in Sulphur Springs, Hopkins County, Texas. She was born on 15 Sep 1895 in Texas. She died on 08 Sep 1984 in Sulphur Springs, Texas.

      More About Julius Leonard Ardis:
      Burial: 01 Jun 1964 in Gafford Chapel Cemetery, Hopkins County, Texas Cause Of Death: Coronary Occlusion

      Notes for Julius Leonard Ardis:
      Headstone has 1887 for year of death. Death certificate has July 12, 1889 for birth date.

iii. VIRGIE JO ARDIS was born on 29 Nov 1892 in Sulphur Springs, Texas. She died on 19 Feb 1962 in Sulphur Springs, Texas. She married Charlie Dow Harris on 25 Sep 1913 in Sulphur Springs, Texas. He was born on 27 Dec 1892 in Texas. He died on 13 Jan 1945 in Cumby, Hopkins county, Texas.

      More About Virgie Jo Ardis:
      Burial: 20 Feb 1962 in Pleasant Grove Cemetery, Cumby, Hopkins County, Texas

Notes for Virgie Jo Ardis:
First name is Virgie on her death certificate. Her first name is Vergoe in her father's obituary.

iv.   OMA FAY ARDIS was born on 26 Mar 1895 in Sulphur Springs, Texas. She died on 13 Mar 1926 in Hopkins County, Texas.

More About Oma Fay Ardis:
Burial: Gafford Chapel Cemetery, Hopkins County, Texas

24.   JULIUS CAESAR[5] ARDIS (Isaac[4], John[3], Isaac[2], Mathias[1]) was born on 02 Feb 1864 in Westville, Alabama. He died on 14 Jul 1937 in Breckenridge, Stephans County, Texas. He married Cora Densmore, daughter of Samuel M. Densmore and Margaret C. (unknown) on 18 Nov 1895 in Eliasville, Texas. She was born on 20 Jan 1870 in Greene County, Tennessee. She died on 17 Nov 1910 in Eliasville, Texas.

More About Julius Caesar Ardis:
Burial: 15 Jul 1937 in Eliasville Cemetery, Eliasville, Texas
Cause Of Death: Cerebral Hemmorhage
Living In: 1930 Living with his brother, Robert Henry Ardis, in Young County, Texas.
Occupation: 1880 in Hopkins County, Texas; Working on his mother's farm.
Occupation: 1900 in Young County, Texas; General Merchandise
Occupation: 1910 in Young County, Texas; Farmer
Occupation: 1920 in Hockley County, Texas; Rail Road Section Laborer
Occupation: 1930 in Eliasville, Texas; Retired
Occupation: Worked for Santa Fe Railroad.

More About Cora Densmore:
Burial: Eliasville Cemetery, Eliasville, Texas

Julius Caesar Ardis and Cora Densmore had the following children:

i.   WILEY B.[6] ARDIS was born on 23 Oct 1896 in Eliasville, Texas. He died on 06 Sep 1897 in Eliasville, Texas.

More About Wiley B. Ardis:
Burial: Eliasville Cemetery, Eliasville, Texas

ii.   JOSEPHINE E. ARDIS was born in Apr 1897 in Eliasville, Texas.

More About Josephine E. Ardis:
Living In: 1920 Living with her father in Hockley County, Texas

iii.   WILLIAM THOMAS ARDIS was born on 19 Sep 1899 in Eliasville, Texas. He died on 19 Jan 1919 in Lubbock, Texas.

More About William Thomas Ardis:
Burial: 20 Jan 1919 in Lubbock, Texas
Cause Of Death: Pneumonia and Influenza
Occupation: Farmer

iv.   SAMUEL KING ARDIS was born on 21 May 1901 in Eliasville, Texas. He died on 23

Apr 1973 in Lubbock, Texas. He married Flora Myrtle Copeland, daughter of Harry Copeland and Pearl Belle Clifford on 28 Aug 1923. She was born on 20 Oct 1906 in Tarrant County, Texas. She died in Lubbock, Texas.

v.　DINKIE D. ARDIS was born on 09 Aug 1904 in Eliasville, Texas. She died on 12 Oct 1982 in Sacramento, California. She married ROY CROW. He was born about 1897 in Harrison, Arkansas.

More About Dinkie D. Ardis:
Burial: Eliasville Cemetery, Eliasville, Texas

Notes for Dinkie D. Ardis:
Social Security death index gives her name as Dee Crow.

vi.　JAMES E. ARDIS was born on 04 May 1908 in Texas. He died on 28 May 1912 in Eliasville, Texas.

More About James E. Ardis:
Burial:　Eliasville　Cemetery,　Eliasville,
Texas
Cause Of Death: Malaria

25.　**MARTHA INEZ[5] ARDIS** (Isaac[4], John[3], Isaac[2], Mathias[1]) was born on 09 Aug 1866 in Greenville, Alabama. She died on 23 Jun 1911 in Lamar County, Texas. She married Thomas H. Marshall, son of John L.Marshall and Susan A. (unknown) on 05 Dec 1883 in Lamar County, Texas. He was born in Aug 1863 in Arkansas.

More About Thomas H. Marshall:
Occupation: 1900 in Hopkins County, Texas; Farmer
Occupation: 1910 in Antlers, Pushmataha County, Oklahoma; Farmer

Thomas H. Marshall and Martha Inez Ardis had the following children:

i.　BERTIE[6] MARSHALL was born in Feb 1886 in Texas.

ii.　NORAH J. MARSHALL was born in Dec 1887 in Texas.

iii.　CLIDE MARSHALL was born in Oct 1889 in Texas.

iv.　ALBERT BECUM MARSHALL was born on 28 Jul 1894 in Sulphur Springs, Texas. He died on 22 Nov 1971 in Modesto, California.

More About Albert Becum Marshall:
Burial:　Acacia　Memorial　Park,　Modesto,　Stanislaus　County,
California
Living In: 1917 in Stephens County, Oklahoma

v.　JOSEPHINE J. MARSHALL was born in Sep 1896 in Texas. She died on 06 May 1936 in Dallas, Dallas County, Texas. She married J. R. WELLS.

vi.　ODELLA MARSHALL was born in May 1899 in Texas.

vii.　ESTELLA MARSHALL was born in May 1899 in Texas.

viii.   BEATRICE MARSHALL was born about 1906 in Indian Territory (present day Oklahoma).

26.   THOMAS ARCHIBALD[5] ARDIS (Archibald McCoy[4], John[3], Isaac[2], Mathias[1]) was born on 03 May 1845 in Salem, Alabama. He died on 18 Feb 1889 in Harrison County, Texas. He married Sarah J. Long, daughter of James D Long and Blanch Ann (unknown) on 08 Nov 1866 in Dale County, Alabama. She was born on 28 May 1846 in Muscogee County, Georgia. She died on 04 Jul 1925 in Ore City, Upshur County, Texas.

More About Thomas Archibald Ardis:
Burial: Clay Hill Cemetery, Fort Rucker, Alabama
Occupation: 1880 in Marshall, Harrison County, Texas; Carpenter
Military Service: Bet. 22 Aug 1863-01 May 1865 ; Company G, 1st Alabama Infantry, C.S.A.

Notes for Thomas Archibald Ardis:
Thomas Archibald Ardis is on a muster roll as present when the 1st Alabama Infantry was surrendered to Major General W. T. Sherman on April 26, 1865 by order of General Joseph E. Johnston, C.S.A.

Enlisted on August 22, 1863 in Perote, Alabama. Paroled at Greensboro, North Carolina May 1, 1865

More About Sarah J. Long:
Burial: Ore City Cemetery, Ore City, Upshur County, Texas
Living In: 1910 Living with her mother in Longview, Gregg County, Texas
Living In: 1920 Living in Texarkana, Arkansas with her son, Augustine, and his wife.

Thomas Archibald Ardis and Sarah J. Long had the following children:

i.   LENORA CORNELIA[6] ARDIS was born on 11 Feb 1869 in Texas. She died on 21 Feb 1937 in Ardmore, Oklahoma. She married Marshall Alvin Richardson on 02 Sep 1886 in Harrison County, Texas. He was born on 25 Nov 1863 in Texas. He died on 29 Sep 1946.

More About Lenora Cornelia Ardis:
Burial: Rose Hill Cemetery, Ardmore, Oklahoma

ii.   THOMAS ARCHIBALD ARDIS was born on 20 Jun 1873 in Longview, Texas. He died on 22 Mar 1945 in Limestone, Illinois. He married HELEN LADEN.

More About Thomas Archibald Ardis:
Burial: 24 Mar 1945 in Lutheran Cemetery, Peoria, Illinois
Occupation: Hotel Clerk

iii.   JAMES LOVE ARDIS was born on 10 Oct 1875 in Gregg County, Texas. He died on 25 Sep 1961 in Dallas, Texas. He married Ella Cornelia Edwards, daughter of C. R. Edwards and Rebecca Williams on 15 Aug 1896 in Anderson County, Texas. She was born on 14 Aug 1878 in Texas. She died on 05 Sep 1956 in University Park,

Dallas County, Texas.

More About James Love Ardis:
Burial: 27 Sep 1961 in Restland Memorial Park, Dallas, Texas
Cause Of Death: Congestive Heart Failure
Living In: 1918 Dallas, Texas
Occupation: Insurance Salesman

 iv. ISAAC MANSFIELD ARDIS was born on 26 Dec 1876 in Longview, Texas. He died on 27 Nov 1932 in San Antonio, Texas. He married JESSIE MAY WYCHE. She was born on 10 May 1882 in Falls County, Texas. She died on 12 May 1933 in Dallas, Texas.

More About Isaac Mansfield Ardis:
Burial: 28 Nov 1932 in Forest Lawn Cemetery, Dallas, Texas
Cause Of Death: Ruptured Duodenal Ulcer
Living In: 1918 in Almena, Kansas
Occupation: Stage Actor
Military Service: Spanish American War

 v. AUGUSTINE WILEY ARDIS was born on 27 May 1879 in Texas. He died on 17 Dec 1941 in Miller County, Arkansas. He married ROBERTA STEGALL. She was born on 29 Aug 1879 in Kansas. She died on 06 Aug 1962 in Arkansas.

More About Augustine Wiley Ardis:
Burial: Woodlawn Cemetery, Texarkana, Arkansas
Living In: 1920 Texarkana, Arkansas

27. **JOHN BLOOMER**[5] **ARDIS** (Archibald McCoy[4], John[3], Isaac[2], Mathias[1]) was born on 23 Dec 1847 in Salem, Alabama. He died on 28 Feb 1900 in Hopkins County, Texas. He married Mary Elizabeth Elliott, daughter of John P. Elliott and Jane Ann Lewis on 24 Dec 1876 in Sulphur Springs, Texas. She was born on 19 Dec 1859 in Hopkins County, Texas. She died on 06 Jun 1899 in Hopkins County, Texas.

More About John Bloomer Ardis:
Burial: Forest Academy Cemetery, Como, Hopkins County, Texas
Occupation: 1880 in Hopkins County, Texas; Farmer

More About Mary Elizabeth Elliott:
Burial: Forest Academy Cemetery, Como, Hopkins County, Texas

John Bloomer Ardis and Mary Elizabeth Elliott had the following children:

 i. HARVEY L.[6] ARDIS was born in 1878 in Hopkins County, Texas.

 ii. ALICE ARDIS was born about 1880 in Hopkins County, Texas. She married WARREN LEWIS.

 iii. RUTH ARDIS was born about 1882 in Hopkins County, Texas.

 iv. ROBERT G. ARDIS was born on 01 Jun 1883. He died on 06 Jun 1886.

More About Robert G. Ardis:

Burial: Forest Academy Cemetery, Hopkins County, Texas

v. L.D. ARDIS was born about 1884 in Hopkins County, Texas.

vi. RUBY ARDIS was born on 21 Jun 1888. She died on 02 Sep 1893.

More About Ruby Ardis:
Burial: Forest Academy Cemetery, Hopkins County, Texas

vii. (UNKNOWN) ARDIS was born on 02 Aug 1890. He died on 20 Aug 1893.

More About (unknown) Ardis:
Burial: Forest Academy Cemetery, Hopkins County, Texas

28. **ISAAC HAMIL**[5] **ARDIS** (Archibald McCoy[4], John[3], Isaac[2], Mathias[1]) was born in Jul 1852 in Salem, Alabama. He died on 14 Feb 1919 in Sulphur Springs, Texas. He married Martha Dennis McCorkle, daughter of Logan Henderson McCorkle and Isabella Zardanik Harper Brown on 24 Dec 1876 in Sulphur Springs, Texas. She was born on 17 Nov 1860 in Hopkins County, Texas. She died on 14 Oct 1934 in Sulphur Springs, Hopkins County, Texas.

More About Isaac Hamil Ardis:
Burial: 15 Dec 1919 in City Cemetery, Sulphur Springs,
Texas
Occupation: 1880 in Hopkins County, Texas; Farmer
Occupation: 1900 in Hopkins County, Texas; Farmer
Occupation: 1910 in Sulphur Springs, Hopkins County, Texas; Running Rooming House

Notes for Isaac Hamil Ardis:
Obit - "I.H. Ardis, one of Sulphur Springs leading citizens for the past quarter of a century, died at his home early Friday morning with paralysis. He had been suffering from previous strokes and his death was not unexpected. Funeral services were held by Elder Bryant and Pastor Moode of the Methodist Church Interment following in the City Cemetery. The deceased was 60 years old and lived nearly all his life in Hopkins County. In 1876, he was united in marriage to Miss Martha McCorkle, who still survives him. In this union, eight children were born, four of whom are still living, as follows: Arch and H.L. Ardis of Dallas, Mrs. Clarence Shaffer of Shreveport, and Allen Ardis now with the US Army in Germany. He is survived by one brother, Love Ardis of this city. (Hopkins Co. Echo, Feb 21, 1919)"

More About Martha Dennis McCorkle:
Burial: 14 Oct 1934 in City Cemetery, Sulphur springs, Hopkins County,
Texas
Living In: 1920 Sulphur Springs, Hopkins County, Texas
Living In: 1930 Sulphur Springs, Hopkins County, Texas

Notes for Martha Dennis McCorkle:
"Mrs. Martha Dennis Ardis, pioneer citizen died at her home on Church street Sunday morning follwing a critical illness of several days. She was the daughter of Mr. & Mrs. L.H. McCorkle who came to Hopkins County from Mississippi and settled the Forest Academy community where they continued to live,and where Mrs. Ardis was born Nov. 17, 1860. She married Isaac H. Ardis in 1876. To this union were born eight children, four of who survive as follows: Arch M. Ardis and Allen E. Ardis of Sulphur Springs, H.L. Ardis of Dallas, and Mrs. Clarence Shaffer of Shreveport,

La. She is also survived by two brothers, R.L. McCorkle of Gladewater and H.C. McCorkle of Sulphur Springs, a half-brother, Alex Harper of Arkansas, two sisters, Mrs. S.A. Hicks of Sulphur Springs and Mrs. M.C. Patman of Chickasha, Okla. She was the sister of the late T.C. McCorkle and Mrs. E.E. Ramey. She joined the Methodist Church at Forest Academy. The family moved to Sulphur Springs 33 yeears ago, and her husband died Feb 14, 1918. Funeral services were held in the First Methodist Church, conducted by Dr. J. Sam Barcus. Burial in the City cemetery. (Hopkins Co. Echo, Oct. 19, 1934)."

Isaac Hamil Ardis and Martha Dennis McCorkle had the following children:

    i.   PEARL B.[6] ARDIS was born in 1878 in Hopkins County, Texas. She died in 1879 in Hopkins County, Texas.

        More About Pearl B. Ardis:
        Burial: Forest Academy Cemetery, Hopkins County, Texas

    ii.   ETHEL IRENA ARDIS was born on 20 Dec 1879 in Hopkins County, Texas. She died on 07 Oct 1892 in Hopkins County, Texas.

        More About Ethel Irena Ardis:
        Burial: Forest Academy Cemetery, Hopkins County, Texas

    iii.   ARCHIBALD MCCORKLE ARDIS was born on 10 Dec 1881 in Hopkins County, Texas. He died on 12 Dec 1950 in Dallas, Texas.

        More About Archibald McCorkle Ardis:
        Burial: 13 Dec 1950 in City Cemetery, Suphur Springs,
        Texas Cause Of Death: Coronary Artery Disease
        Living In: 1918 Dallas, Texas
        Living In: 1942 Dallas, Texas
        Occupation: Retail Dry Goods Salesman

        Notes   for   Archibald   McCorkle
        Ardis: Never married.

    iv.   JOHN HAMEL ARDIS was born on 09 Aug 1884 in Hopkins County, Texas. He died on 21 Jan 1893.

        More About John Hamel Ardis:
        Burial: Forest Academy Cemetery, Hopkins County, Texas

    v.   ALLEN EDWARD ARDIS was born on 13 Aug 1887 in Hopkins County, Texas. He died on 23 Apr 1966 in Texas.

        More About Allen Edward Ardis:
        Burial: City Cemetery, Sulphur Springs, Texas
        Living In: 1910 Living with his parents in Sulphur Springs, Texas.
        Living In: 1920 Living with his mother in Sulphur Springs, Texas.
        Living In: 1930 Living with his mother in Sulphur Springs, Texas.
        Occupation: 1917 in Sulphur Springs, Hopkins County, Texas; Dry Goods Clerk
        Occupation: 1920 in Sulphur Springs, Hopkins County, Texas; Travelling Salesman

for Wholesale Dry Goods
Occupation: 1930 in Sulphur Springs, Hopkins County, Texas; Dry Goods
Clerk
Occupation: 1940 in Sulphur Springs, Hopkins County, Texas; Mayor
Military Service: World War One - France; 315th Engineers, 90th Division,
U.S. Army

vi. SUSIE MAY ARDIS was born on 14 Dec 1889 in Hopkins County, Texas. She died
on 10 Oct 1894.

More About Susie May Ardis:
Burial: Forest Academy Cemetery, Hopkins County, Texas

vii. HENRY LEROY ARDIS was born on 01 Aug 1892 in Hopkins County, Texas. He died
on 12 Aug 1987 in Dallas, Texas. He married ILA MAE (UNKNOWN). She was born
on 19 Oct 1900 in Oklahoma. She died on 18 May 1997 in Collin County, Texas.

More About Henry Leroy Ardis:
Burial: Restland Memorial Park, Dallas, Texas

viii. MATTIE LOU ARDIS was born on 03 Aug 1896 in Hopkins County, Texas. She died
in May 1983 in Caddo Parish, Louisiana. She married Clarence H. Shaffer on 23
Jun 1914 in Sulphur Springs, Hopkins County, Texas. He was born about 1886 in
Texas.

29. **HENRY LOVE**[5] **ARDIS** (Archibald McCoy[4], John[3], Isaac[2], Mathias[1]) was born on 12 Sep 1857 in
Pike County, Alabama. He died on 06 Jan 1927 in Sulphur Springs, Texas. He married Martha
Pate, daughter of John W. Pate and Sarah A. Wester on 02 Dec 1880 in Sulphur Springs, Texas.
She was born on 20 Sep 1863 in Hopkins County, Texas. She died on 27 Jan 1952 in Sulphur
Springs, Texas.

More About Henry Love Ardis:
Burial: City Cemetery, Sulphur Springs, Texas
Living In: 10 Jun 1880 Living with his brother, Isaac Hamil Ardis, in Hopkins County, Texas
Occupation: 1880 in Hopkins County, Texas; Farmer
Occupation: 1900 in Hopkins County, Texas; (can not read census information for
occupation)
Occupation: 1910 in Sulphur Springs, Hopkins County, Texas; Farmer
Occupation: 1920; Retail Grocery Merchant, Sulphur Springs, Texas

More About Martha Pate:
Burial: 28 Jan 1952 in City Cemetery, Sulphur Springs, Texas
Cause Of Death: Pulmonary Embolism and Bronchitis.
Living In: 1930 Sulphur Springs, Hopkins County, Texas
Living In: 1940 Living with her daughter, Sallie, in Sulphur Springs, Texas

Notes for Martha Pate:
Death Certificate gives 9/20/1863 as date of birth.

Henry Love Ardis and Martha Pate had the following children:

i. ZULA[6] ARDIS was born on 30 Sep 1881 in Texas. She died on 04 May 1961 in
Sulphur Springs, Texas. She married WILLIE ESTER MELTON. He was born on
23 Oct 1877 in Texas. He died on 11 Sep 1949 in Sulphur Springs, Texas.

More About Zula Ardis:
Burial: 05 May 1961 in City Cemetery, Sulphur Springs, Texas
Cause Of Death: Acute Coronary Thrombosis

ii.	SALLIE ARDIS was born on 03 Aug 1883 in Sulphur Springs, Texas. She died on 08 Apr 1959 in Sulphur Springs, Texas. She married James Luther Hutcherson on 18 Feb 1904 in Hopkins County, Texas. He was born on 03 Aug 1880 in Georgia. He died on 21 Oct 1946 in Texas.

More About Sallie Ardis:
Burial: 09 Apr 1959 in Sulphur Springs City Cemetery, Sulphur Springs, Texas Cause Of Death: ; Cancer
Living In: 1920 Sallie and her children are living with her parents in Sulphur Springs, Texas.
Living In: 1930 Sallie and her son, James, are living with her mother in Sulphur Springs, Texas
Occupation: 1930 in Sulphur Springs, Hopkins County, Texas; Dressmaker with her own shop.
Occupation: 1940 in Sulphur Springs, Hopkins County, Texas; Beauty Shop Attendant
Occupation: 1959 in Sulphur Springs, Hopkins County, Texas; Gift Shop Owner

iii.	NORA ARDIS was born on 10 Nov 1885 in Sulphur Springs, Texas. She died on 13 Dec 1977 in Texas. She married James William Weaver on 24 Sep 1906 in Hopkins County, Texas. He was born on 03 Apr 1882. He died on 04 Nov 1968 in Texas.

More About Nora Ardis:
Burial: Sulphur Springs City Cemetery, Sulphur Springs, Texas

iv.	OSCAR GRADY ARDIS was born on 27 Jun 1889 in Eliasville, Texas. He died on 12 Nov 1969 in Sulphur Springs, Texas. He married Lura Higdon, daughter of Hubert Higdon and Agnes Thornton on 02 Nov 1912. She was born on 01 Nov 1892 in Hopkins County, Texas. She died on 18 Feb 1972 in Farmers Branch, Dallas County, Texas.

More About Oscar Grady Ardis:
Burial: 14 Nov 1969 in City Cemetery, Sulphur Springs, Hopkins County, Texas
Cause Of Death: Pneumonia and Parkinson's Disease
Occupation: 1910 in Sulphur Springs, Hopkins, Texas, USA; Hardware Salesman
Occupation: Dairyman

v.	AMANDA FAYE ARDIS was born on 04 Oct 1892 in Eliasville, Texas. She died on 11 Apr 1981 in Hopkins County, Texas. She married Henry Leroy Davis, son of James Harvey Davis and Belle Barton on 29 Dec 1915 in Hopkins County, Texas. He was born on 20 Apr 1891 in Mt. Vernon, Franklin County, Texas. He died on 21 Jun 1952 in Sulphur Springs, Hopkins County, Texas.

More About Amanda Faye Ardis:
Burial: Sulphur Springs City Cemetery, Sulphur Springs, Texas

vi.	JACK ARDIS was born on 14 Mar 1894 in Alvin, Texas. He died on 16 Feb 1974 in Sulphur Springs, Texas. He married DORA BERNICE TAYLOR. She was born on 19

Sep 1902. She died on 10 Jul 1973.

More About Jack Ardis:
Burial: 17 Feb 1974 in City Cemetery, Sulphur Springs, Texas
Living In: 1920 Living with his parents in Sulphur Springs, Texas
Occupation: 1920 in Sulphur Springs, Hopkins County, Texas; Bakery
Merchant Military Service: World War One

vii.   LOUIS EDWARD ARDIS was born on 18 Apr 1897 in Sulphur Springs, Texas. He died on 02 Feb 1972 in Dallas, Texas. He married THELMA PRATT. She was born on 26 Aug 1905 in Texas. She died on 12 Dec 1962 in Sulphur Springs, Texas. He married SYBIL FRANCES FERGUSON. She was born on 01 Jul 1902. She died on 15 Jun 1990.

More About Louis Edward Ardis:
Burial: 02 Feb 1972 in City Cemetery, Suphur Springs, Texas
Cause Of Death: Respiratory Failure due to Emphysema
Living In: 1920 Living with his parents in Sulphur Springs, Texas
Occupation: 1920 in Sulphur Springs, Hopkins County, Texas; Freight Agent
Occupation: Oilman

Notes for Louis Edward Ardis:
Death Certificate has the signature of Sybil Ardis(wife) as informant.

viii.   ABLE BOYET ARDIS was born on 14 Oct 1899 in Alvin, Texas. He died on 28 Feb 1986. He married MARIE CONNER HARRIS. She was born on 14 Jun 1904. She died on 27 Aug 1999.

More About Able Boyet Ardis:
Burial: City Cemetery, Sulphur Springs, Texas

30.   **JOHN ARDIS**[5] **PACE** (Caroline Columbia Sarah Ann Collingsworth[4] Ardis, John[3] Ardis, Isaac[2] Ardis, Mathias[1] Ardis) was born on 09 Apr 1838 in Harris County, Georgia. He died on 02 Jul 1909 in Ennis, Texas. He married (1) **ELIZA FRAZIER** on 04 Dec 1860 in Russell County, Alabama. She was born in Alabama. He married (2) **LEVINIA R. (UNKNOWN)** about 1876. She was born on 12 Dec 1840 in Alabama. She died on 09 Feb 1915 in Ennis, Texas.

More About John Ardis Pace:
Burial: Myrtle Cemetery, Ennis, Ellis County, Texas
Living In: 1900 Ennis, Ellis County, Texas
Occupation: 1880 in Ellis County, Texas; Grocery Merchant
Occupation: 1900 in Ennis, Ellis County, Texas; Merchant
Occupation: Minister

John Ardis Pace and Eliza Frazier had the following children:

i.   MARTHA IDA[6] PACE was born on 04 Jan 1862 in Opelika, Alabama. She died on 03 Jul 1951 in Lancaster, Dallas County, Texas. She married Andrew C. King on 21 Apr 1881 in Ellis County. Texas. He was born on 25 Oct 1858. He died on 03 Dec 1884 in Ennis, Texas.

More About Martha Ida Pace:
Burial: 05 Jul 1951 in Myrtle Cemetery, Ennis, Ellis County, Texas
Cause Of Death: Uremia due to Congestive Heart Failure
Living In: 1900 Ida, as a widow, and her daughter Hattie are living with Ida's father and step mother in Ennis, Texas
Living In: 1910 Living with her daughter, Hattie, and son in law in Quanah, Texas
Living In: 1920 Living with her daughter, Hattie, and son in law in Quanah, Texas
Living In: 1930   Dallas, Texas

    ii.   WILLIAM ISAAC PACE was born on 19 Mar 1864 in Alabama. He died on 28 Jan 1939 in Dallas, Texas. He married Amanda Gatewood, daughter of Benjamin Dudley Gatewood and Amanda B. Buchanan on 24 Feb 1886. She was born on 03 Dec 1864 in Texas. She died on 05 Apr 1951 in Greely, Colorado.

        More About William Isaac Pace:
        Burial: 30 Jan 1939 in Restland Memorial Park, Dallas, Texas
        Occupation: Merchant

    iii.   LOLA PACE was born about 1866 in Alabama.

More About Levinia R. (unknown):
Burial: Myrtle Cemetery, Ennis, Ellis County, Texas
Living In: 1910 Living in Ennis, Texas as a lodger in the household of Abe Carroll.

31.   STEPHEN A.[5] PACE (Caroline Columbia Sarah Ann Collingsworth[4] Ardis, John[3] Ardis, Isaac[2] Ardis, Mathias[1] Ardis) was born on 19 Sep 1848 in Columbus, Muscogee County, Georgia. He died on 01 Mar 1921 in Corsicana, Navarro County, Texas. He married Achsah Eugenia Maddux on 05 Dec 1870 in Freestone, Texas. She was born on 26 Aug 1849 in Alabama. She died on 30 Mar 1901 in Corsicana, Navarro County, Texas.

More About Stephen A. Pace:
Burial: 02 Mar 1921 in Oakwood Cemetery, Corsicana, Navarro County, Texas
Occupation: 1880 in Corsicana, Navarro County, Texas; Wholesale and Retail Grocer
Occupation: 1900 in Corsicana, Navarro County, Texas; Wholesale Grocer
Occupation: 1910 in Corsicana, Navarro County, Texas; Wholesale Grocery Merchant
Occupation: 1920 in Corsicana, Navarro County, Texas; Grocery Merchant

More About Achsah Eugenia Maddux:
Burial: Oakwood Cemetery, Corsicana, Navarro County, Texas

Stephen A. Pace and Achsah Eugenia Maddux had the following children:

    i.   THERESA C.[6] PACE was born on 12 Jan 1873 in Texas. She died on 28 Feb 1933 in Corsicana, Navarro County, Texas. She married RICHARD MAYS. He was born on 28 Mar 1866 in Florida. He died on 06 Jan 1946 in Corsicana, Navarro County, Texas.

        More About Theresa C. Pace:
        Burial: Oakwood Cemetery, Corsicana, Navarro County, Texas

    ii.   PAULINE PACE was born on 12 Mar 1879 in Texas. She died on 26 Nov 1917 in Texas. She married JACK WOMACK. He was born on 05 Jun 1860 in Texas. He died on 08 Aug 1934 in Mexia, Limestone County, Texas.

More About Pauline Pace:
Burial: Oakwood Cemetery, Corsicana, Navarro County, Texas

iii. LOUISE AUGUSTA PACE was born on 16 Jan 1881 in Texas. She died on 24 Nov 1957 in Texas. She married (UNKNOWEN) KING.

More About Louise Augusta Pace:
Burial: Oakwood Cemetery, Corsicana, Navarro County, Texas
Living In: 1910 Living with her father in Corsicana, Texas.
Living In: 1920 Living with her father in Corsicana, Texas.

iv. STEPHEN PACE was born in Dec 1882 in Texas. He died on 04 Dec 1907 in Corsicana, Navarro County, Texas.

More About Stephen Pace:
Burial: Oakwood Cemetery, Corsicana, Navarro County, Texas

v. HOMER PACE was born on 17 Feb 1887 in Texas. He died on 08 Jul 1952 in Corsicana, Navarro County, Texas.

More About Homer Pace:
Burial: 09 Jul 1952 in Oakwood Cemetery, Corsicana, Navarro County, Texas Cause Of Death: Cerebral Hemorrhage
Living In: 1910 Living with his father in Corsicana, Texas
Occupation: Grocery Salesman

32. JOHN JESSE^5 SCAIFE (Martha Aly D.^{4} Ardis, John^3 Ardis, Isaac^2 Ardis, Mathias^1 Ardis) was born on 2 May 1852 in Alabama. He died on 20 Apr 1921 in Louisiana. He married ALLIE EALY BROWN. She was born on 10 Oct 1860 in Alabama. She died on 07 Dec 1921 in Louisiana.

More About John Jesse Scaife:
Burial: Old Leesville Cemetery, Leesville, Vernon Parish, Louisiana
Occupation: 1880 in Pensacola, Florida; Teamster
Occupation: 1900 in Vernon Parish, Louisiana; Day Laborer

More About Allie Ealy Brown:
Burial: Old Leesville Cemetery, Leesville, Vernon Parish, Louisiana

John Jesse Scaife and Allie Ealy Brown had the following child:

i. WILLIAM TERRY^6 SCAIFE was born on 30 May 1879 in Alabama. He died on 19 May 1908 in Louisiana.

More About William Terry Scaife:
Burial: Old Leesville Cemetery, Leesville, Vernon Parish, Louisiana
Occupation: 1900 in Vernon Parish, Louisiana; Shoemaker

33. JOANNA^5 ARDIS (Nebraska Kansas^4, John^3, Isaac^2, Mathias^1) was born on 11 Mar 1882 in Starlington, Butler County, Alabama. She died on 19 Jan 1962 in Austin, Texas. She married Allen Henry Benson, son of William H. Benson and Nancy C. Reid on 01 Apr 1900. He was born on 10 Sep 1879 in Alabama. He died on 26 Jul 1945 in Austin, Texas.

More About Joanna Ardis:
Living In: 1930 Mobile, Alabama with her children. Her husband is not on this census listing.
Living In: 1961 Houston, Texas

More About Allen Henry Benson:
Burial: Perdido Baptist Church Cemetery, Perdido, Alabama
Cause Of Death: Chronic Nephritis
Living In: Bet. 1900-1920 Conecuh County, Alabama
Occupation: Farmer

Notes for Allen Henry Benson:
Headstone has September 10, 1879 for date of birth. 1900 U.S. census has September 1879 for date of birth. Death certificate has September 10, 1879 for date of birth. World War One draft registration has September 10, 1878 for date of birth.

Allen Henry Benson and Joanna Ardis had the following children:

    i.   WILLIE BELLE[6] BENSON was born about 1902 in Alabama.

    ii.   GERTRUDE BENSON was born about 1905 in Alabama.

    iii.   JOHN HOWARD BENSON was born on 15 Sep 1907 in Conecuh County, Alabama. He died on 28 Jul 1947 in Texas City, Texas.

        More About John Howard Benson:
        Burial: Perdido Baptist Church Cemetery, Perdido, Alabama Cause Of Death: Fell from an oil tank
        Occupation: Boiler Maker

        Notes for John Howard Benson:
        Headstone has September 15, 1907 for date of birth. Death certificate has September 15, 1908 for date of birth.

    iv.   EDGAR BENSON was born about 1911 in Alabama.

        More About Edgar Benson:
        Occupation: 1930 - Boilermaker in shipyard

    v.   GRACE BENSON was born about 1914 in Alabama.

    vi.   ELOISE BENSON was born about 1919 in Alabama.

34.   **JOHNNIE ELIZABETH[5] ARDIS** (Nebraska Kansas[4], John[3], Isaac[2], Mathias[1]) was born on 18 Jan 1887 in Conecuh County, Alabama. She died on 13 Aug 1968 in Mobile, Alabama. She married Louis Claude Havard on 11 Dec 1905. He was born on 30 Jan 1886 in Perdido, Alabama. He died on 11 Apr 1931 in Mobile, Alabama.

More About Johnnie Elizabeth Ardis:
Burial: 13 Aug 1968 in Perdido Baptist Church Cemetery, Perdido, Alabama

More About Louis Claude Havard:

Burial: Perdido Baptist Church Cemetery, Perdido, Alabama

Louis Claude Havard and Johnnie Elizabeth Ardis had the following children:

    i.   EUGENE F.[6] HAVARD was born in 1912. He died in 1928.

    ii.   JASPER W. HAVARD was born in 1918. He died in 2004.

35.   JOHN K.[5] ARDIS (Nebraska Kansas[4], John[3], Isaac[2], Mathias[1]) was born on 20 Apr 1918 in Perdido, Alabama. He married Vivian Ruth Smith on 24 Sep 1937 in Alabama. She was born about 1918 in Alabama.

More About John K. Ardis:
Living In: 1940 Living, with his wife and child, in the home of his mother in Perdido, Alabama.
Occupation: 1940 in Perdido, Baldwin County, Alabama; Truck Driver

John K. Ardis and Vivian Ruth Smith had the following child:

    i.   JOHN W.[6] ARDIS was born about 1939 in Alabama.

36.   ISAAC[5] ARDIS (William Trammell[4], John[3], Isaac[2], Mathias[1]) was born on 03 Nov 1898 in Mississippi. He died on 03 Feb 1973 in Frisco City, Monroe County, Alabama. He married MAGGIE MARSHALL. She was born on 15 May 1895. She died on 09 Oct 1988.

More About Isaac Ardis:
Burial: Mineola Cemetery, Uriah, Alabama

More About Maggie Marshall:
Burial: Mineola Cemetery, Uriah, Alabama

Isaac Ardis and Maggie Marshall had the following child:

    i.   ANNETTE[6] ARDIS was born on 05 Aug 1932. Annette died on 19 Apr 1933.

        More About Annette Ardis:
        Burial: Mineola Cemetery, Uriah, Alabama